THE STATE AND THE ECONOMY UNDER CAPITALISM

FUNDAMENTALS OF PURE AND APPLIED ECONOMICS

EDITORS IN CHIEF

J. LESOURNE, Conservatoire National des Arts et Métiers, Paris, France

H. SONNENSCHEIN, University of Pennsylvania, Philadelphia, PA, USA

ADVISORY BOARD

K. ARROW, Stanford, CA, USA
W. BAUMOL, Princeton, NJ, USA
W. A. LEWIS, Princeton, NJ, USA
S. TSURU, Tokyo, Japan

MARXIAN ECONOMICS II
In 3 Volumes

THE STATE AND THE ECONOMY UNDER CAPITALISM

ADAM PRZEWORSKI

First published in 1990 by
Routledge

Reprinted in 2001 by
Routledge
2 Park Square, Milton Park, Abingdon, Oxfordshire OX14 4RN
711 Third Avenue, New York, NY 10017
First issued in paperback 2014
Routledge is an imprint of the Taylor and Francis Group, an informa business

Transferred to Digital Printing 2007

© 1990 Routledge

The publishers have made every effort to contact authors/copyright holders
of the works reprinted in *Fundamentals of Pure & Applied Economics*.
This has not been possible in every case, however, and we would welcome
correspondence from those individuals/companies we have been unable to
trace.

These reprints are taken from original copies of each book. in many cases
the condition of these originals is not perfect. the publisher has gone to
great lengths to ensure the quality of these reprints, but wishes to point
out that certain characteristics of the original copies will, of necessity, be
apparent in reprints thereof.

British Library Cataloguing in Publication Data
A CIP catalogue record for this book
is available from the British Library

The State and the Economy under Capitalism
ISBN 978-0-415-26990-2 (hbk)
ISBN 978-0-415-51098-1 (pbk)
Marxian Economics II: 3 Volumes
ISBN 978-0-415-26987-2

Contents

Introduction to the Series

Drawing on a personal network, an economist can still relatively easily stay well informed in the narrow field in which he works, but to keep up with the development of economics as a whole is a much more formidable challenge. Economists are confronted with difficulties associated with the rapid development of their discipline. There is a risk of "balkanization" in economics, which may not be favorable to its development.

Fundamentals of Pure and Applied Economics has been created to meet this problem. The discipline of economics has been subdivided into sections (listed at the back of this volume). These sections comprise short books, each surveying the state of the art in a given area.

Each book starts with the basic elements and goes as far as the most advanced results. Each should be useful to professors needing material for lectures, to graduate students looking for a global view of a particular subject, to professional economists wishing to keep up with the development of their science, and to researchers seeking convenient information on questions that incidentally appear in their work.

Each book is thus a presentation of the state of the art in a particular field rather than a step-by-step analysis of the development of the literature. Each is a high-level presentation but accessible to anyone with a solid background in economics, whether engaged in business, government, international organizations, teaching, or research in related fields.

Three aspects of *Fundamentals of Pure and Applied Economics* should be emphasized:

—First, the project covers the whole field of economics, not only theoretical or mathematical economics.
—Second, the project is open-ended and the number of books is not predetermined. If new interesting areas appear, they will generate additional books.

—Last, all the books making up each section will later be grouped to constitute one or several volumes of an Encyclopedia of Economics.

The editors of the sections are outstanding economists who have selected as authors for the series some of the finest specialists in the world.

J. Lesourne   *H. Sonnenschein*

The State and the Economy under Capitalism*

ADAM PRZEWORSKI
University of Chicago

INTRODUCTION

Capitalism is a system in which scarce resources are owned privately. Yet under capitalism property is institutionally separated from authority. As a result, there are two mechanisms by which resources are allocated to uses and distributed to households: the market and the state. In the market, productive resources — capital, land, labor capacities — are allocated by their owners and the distribution of consumption results from decentralized interactions. Yet the state can also allocate and distribute and it can act on those same resources that constitute private property. Not only can states tax and transfer but they can regulate the relative costs and benefits associated with private decisions. Thus, inherent in capitalism is a permanent tension between the market and the state.

Democracy in the political realm exacerbates this tension. The market is a mechanism in which individual agents cast votes for allocations with the resources they own and these resources are always distributed unequally; democracy is a system through which people as citizens may express preferences about allocating resources that they do not own, with rights distributed more equally. Hence the two mechanisms can lead to the same outcome only by a fluke. Indeed, distributions of consumption caused by the market and those collectively preferred by citizens must be systematically different since democracy offers those who are poor, oppressed or otherwise miserable as a consequence of the private ownership of productive resources an apportunity to find redress via the state.

*This work has been supported in part by grants from the National Science Foundation and a Fellowship from the German Marshall Fund.

1

The perennial issue of political theory, and of practical politics, concerns the competence of these two mechanisms with regard to each other. Is it possible for governments to control a capitalist economy? In particular, is it possible to steer the economy against interests and preferences of those who control the productive wealth?

Since these questions involve interests and values, logical and empirical arguments are closely intertwined with normative and political concerns. The proper role of the state with regard to various aspects of social and economic life constitutes the central issue of contemporary political controversies. Should governments intervene in the economy at all? Do states fill functional gaps in markets, thus rendering resource allocation more efficient? Are markets operating smoothly only because they are organized and continually regulated by states? Or is state intervention always a source of uncertainty and inefficiency? On balance, is it beneficial or detrimental for general welfare? Are states universalistically minded organizations pursuing the general interest or are they just another among the multitude of particularistic actors, distinguished only by the monopoly of coercion?

The issues raised by the uneasy co-existence of states and markets are so generic that they re-emerge in academic fields which have no common substantive interests. Studies of public policy have proliferated to the point that journals are published these days in specialized fields such as housing policy, policy towards the arts, fiscal policy, defense policy or industrial policy. Yet, while each of these areas undoubtedly comprises some specialized technical aspects, theoretical debates arrive at the same issues and become organized by the same positions regardless of the substantive problematic.

The basic theoretical positions are three: states respond to preferences of citizens, states pursue goals of their own, states act in the interest of those who own productive wealth. In the first view, people rule. "The people," in the eighteenth century singular, exercises its sovereignty through the democratic process. Politicians, who compete for political support, offer those policies which are collectively preferred by citizens and, once in office, pursue these policies. Governments are thus perfect agents of the public. In the second view, states are institutions autonomous from societies. States rule: governments pursue policies which reflect values or interests of state managers. Finally, in the third perspective, states are so constrained by the economy, specifically by interests of private owners of productive resources, that governments cannot and do not undertake any actions contrary to these interests. Hence, it is "capital" that rules.

None of these theoretical perspectives, and the political programmes they inspire, are new. Questions concerning the democratic method dominated political debates at the time of the American and French Revolutions. The view that the democratic process is inherently imperfect and inferior to the market as a mechanism for allocating resources dates back to Burke and de Maistre: the end of the eighteenth century. The fear of any specialized political institutions, even representative ones, goes back to Rousseau and has a convoluted ideological history: originally a left-wing theme, anti-statism was only recently, and only in its economic aspect, embraced by the Right. Finally, the belief that popular sovereignty is gravely curtailed in any society in which productive resources are owned privately has been the traditional, almost defining, feature of socialist movements.

Yet the fact that all the current positions have their roots in the period when the modern political and economic institutions had been forged, does not mean that we have made no progress. Pages that follow testify that traditional arguments have benefited from the newly developed analytical apparatus. Assumptions have been clarified, arguments have been organized in deductive models, rival empirical hypotheses have been drawn. Assertions have been replaced by arguments; normative standards have become explicit and quite technical; evidence shifted from anecdotal to systematic. One can hold different ideological positions and yet argue: this is the transformation made possible by the adoption of a standard technical language. True, empirical evidence continues to be scant and many issues cannot be decided by reference to evidence. Yet ideological disagreements have been rationalized.

The three major views of the relation between states and economies constitute the subject of this monograph.

Part I is devoted to two questions: whether the democratic process provides a unique reading of individual preferences and whether democracy leads to efficient economic outcomes? The assumptions and the logical structure of economic theories of democracy are briefly outlined, with the focus on the relation between theories of social choice and of the democratic state. Neo-liberal theories, which maintain that governments inevitably cause inefficiency, are then reconstructed and subjected to an internal critique. Finally, external criticisms of this approach are summarized, particularly those which emphasize the corporatist organization of interests.

After some terminological preliminaries, Part II is organized around four questions: How frequently and to what extent are states autonomous? What conditions promote state autonomy? What are the consequences of different forms of state autonomy for government policies? How do bureaucrats and politicians manage to become autonomous under democratic conditions? The traditional marxist view of state autonomy as contingent on class relations is juxtaposed to the "state-centric" approach which takes state autonomy as a methodological postulate. The analysis of the consequences of different forms of autonomy is based on the neo-classical approach to economic history. Finally, models of autonomous bureaus and legislatures under democracy are placed within the context of institutional and economic constraints.

Part III centers on the two questions posed by marxist theories of the state: Is the survival of capitalism due to interventions by the state? Why is it that governments act to foster capitalism? The logic of functionalist marxist theories of state is reconstructed first, followed by two important versions of this theory. The entire approach is then subjected to a critique that emphasizes both empirical and logical problems confronted by this approach. Finally, game-theoretic models which place government policies within the context of class conflict are reviewed as an alternative approach to the marxist problematic.

The concluding pages (Part IV) return to political issues.

Part I: The Rule of the People

1. INTRODUCTION

Economic theories of democracy explain policies of governments by preferences of individuals. The general structure of these theories is the following. There are individuals, who reveal through some procedures their preferences for government policies. There are teams of actual and rival politicians who compete for political support. Support maximizing candidates offer policies collectively preferred by citizens and they pursue these policies once in office. Governments are thus perfect agents of the public.

The people to whom governments respond are typically identified only as "individuals," that is, all preferences are a priori possible and all coalitions among them are equally likely. Individuals are rational in the sense that they support those policy proposals and those governments which come closest to maximizing their welfare. Individuals reveal their preferences through a variety of mechanisms, ranging from voting in elections to bribing bureaucrats. In turn, state managers — elected politicians, nominated bureaucrats, or more abstractly "the regulator" — are led to do what people want them to do by their own interests because they compete for popular support.

This happy coincidence between collective preferences and government policies breaks down if any of several conditions does not hold: if no unique collective choice exists, if the preference revealing mechanism induces individuals to anticipate each other's actions in ways that are collectively suboptimal, if state managers do not compete, or if they cannot be effectively supervised. But even if governments are perfectly responsive to collective choices, a question emerges whether policies that enjoy most support are indeed best for the individuals who grant this support, that is, whether the state should intervene in the economy even in ways that respond to the collective preference.

The relation between government policies and preferences of individuals provides the subject of Section 2. To clarify the assumptions, we begin in Section 2.1. with a case in which citizens are homogeneous and there is no state to speak of. We then focus, in Section 2.2, on the model of situations in which citizens with similarly structured preferences vote by majority rule on a particular issue: "the median voter model." To close this analysis, we briefly summarize in Section 2.3. the main reason the optimistic results of the median voter model may not hold. The subject of Section 3 is the question whether the state even intervenes in the economy in the best interest of individuals, even when it is perfectly responsive to their revealed preferences. Section 3.1. presents the views of the (Chicago) school of regulation; it is followed in 3.2 by a critical review of this model. A brief overview closes this Part.

2. MAJORITY RULE

2.1. Homogeneous citizens

To understand the logic of these theories and the questions which they pose, consider an ideal democracy. In this system all citizens have equal income and wealth, and they all vote simultaneously, choosing from a single dimension the level of a government activity. Suppose that merchants of Venice face the choice of how many convoy ships they should build to protect their commercial vessels from pirates. Each citizen seeks to maximize his net benefit from government activities, that is, each votes for the level of activities which maximizes the difference between benefits and costs. The level of protection which is efficient is the level for which the marginal benefit equals the marginal cost. Hence Venetian merchants vote to fund just so many convoy ships that the last one added exactly pays for itself in the benefits of additional protection it provides. It would make no sense for them not to add this ship since the one before still contributed more in protection than in cost; it would make no sense to build more than this ship because the next one would cost more than it contributes.

Thus homogeneous citizens would choose a level of activity that is efficient for each and all. They would then charge themselves the per capita cost of this decision. Once the number of ships is decided upon, citizens accept competitive bids for building the ships. Competition brings the price of services to the level which represents the true cost to the provider: cost which was known to citizens when they calculated marginal costs and benefits. The state would be a perfect agent under these conditions since the state is nothing but the citizens themselves; there is no state to speak of.

Note that since the same policy is optimal for every citizen, all voting rules would generate the same outcome. Moreover, transforming this direct democracy into a representative system would not change anything. Suppose that there exists a public office of the Contractor, who decides on the level of activity and contracts it out. Candidates for this office compete with each other; the candidate who is closer to the policy preferred by the citizens wins over his opponent; to maximize support, that is, to win the election, all candidates converge to the collective preference.

Thus, when citizens are homogeneous, the political process yields a unique outcome. If candidates for office compete with each other and if government services are provided competitively, then the state functions efficiently as a perfect agent of the public.

2.2. Median voter models

Perhaps surprisingly, the basic features of this perfect democracy survive in a world in which individuals differ in endowments, incomes, and preferences and in which decisions are made by the majority rule. This is the central conclusion of the median voter models.

Suppose now that each citizen has some endowments, such as wealth and labor, an income which accrues to these endowments when they are gainfully utilized, and preferences over a number of dimensions, such as consumption, leisure, public goods, or welfare of others. These preferences are such that one outcome is preferred over all others and as the distance between the most preferred outcome and any alternative increases, the utility of each individual does not increase ("single-peaked preferences"). For most of this section it will be useful to think of individuals as ordered in a twofold manner: from the poorest (in endowments or in income) to the richest and from most opposed to most favorable to some outcome to be decided by the political process.

Individuals vote to decide the level of government activities, which may comprise providing a public good or effecting a pure transfer of income. The issue which is being decided is to choose a particular value or values from one dimension. Thus the question may concern the number of ships to be built for protection, the budget of a school district, the age of legal drinking, the number of legal holidays, or the amount of unemployment compensations. Each individual can submit a proposal for quantity; each proposal is paired against the status quo; voting is instantaneous, universal, and costless.

Decisions are made by the majority rule. The winner, if there is one, is the proposal which no alternative can defeat in a pairwise majority vote (majority rule equilibrium).

When these and several additional conditions hold, the following three propositions are true:

(1) One policy proposal is a unique winner and this is the proposal most preferred by the voter with the median preference [Bowen, 1943; Black, 1958; Davis and Hinich, 1966; Kramer, 1973.]

(2) When all voters vote or when the distribution of preferences in the electorate is unimodal and symmetric and if two and only two

parties compete to win elections, both parties converge to the position most favored by the voter with the median preference [Hotelling, 1929; Downs, 1957; Davis, Hinich, and Ordeshook, 1970][1]*

(3) When some additional conditions are satisfied — to be discussed below — the voter with the median preference is the one with the median income. [Foley, 1967; Roberts, 1977].

These three propositions together constitute the "median voter model." The first theorem specifies the majority equilibrium: the result of direct vote by majority rule. The second asserts that if such an equilibrium exists and if two parties compete, the majority equilibrium will be the winning electoral platform. The third theorem narrows the scope of the theory to issues in which preference orderings have something to do with income (or endowments which determine income). Thus the first theorem concerns a model of voting in a committee; the first two propositions jointly specify the outcome of party competition; in turn, the first and the third theorems combined provide a model of voting in committees on issues in which income distribution plays a role. The full model specifies, therefore, the outcome of competition between two parties on issues which involve income. In fact, the first two theorems are of central interest to the theory of social choice, while the theory of government role with regard to the economy follows specifically from the inclusion of the third theorem. We will thus neglect all the technical aspects involved in the first two theorems and focus on one particular class of models which involve taxation and distribution of income or provision of public goods.

We are now dealing, therefore, only with the following situations. Voting concerns the rate of taxation to be imposed on incomes. Any tax schedule can be proposed, as long as incomes of the same magnitude are taxed at the same rate and the tax rate is (weakly) monotonically related to income. The revenue which is collected through the tax is spent either on some pure public good, which is equally appreciated by all voters, or it is distributed equally to all voters.[2] Thus the cost of the proposal to each individual depends upon his/her pre-tax income while the benefit is the same regardless of income. Net benefit or cost is thus related to the original income.

Without imposing any additional restrictions, examine the situation

*The Notes section is to be found at the end of the text.

from the point of view of an individual voter, *i*, who has some pre-fisc (that is, pre-tax, pre-transfer) income $Y(i)$. The optimal tax schedule for this voter will be the one in which everyone with incomes smaller and equal to $Y(i)$ pays no taxes and everyone with higher incomes pays the entire income in taxes [Kramer and Synder, 1983]. Let the electorate consist of three voters: Wealthy, Median, and Poor [or $(n + 1)$ voters, $n/2$ wealthy, the median voter, and $n/2$ poor], with pre-vote incomes $Y(W) > Y(M) > Y(P)$. Note first that the voter with the median income has the median preference concerning the tax rate: Wealthy would want the tax rate to be zero throughout, Poor would want it to jump to one at an income infinitesimally larger than hers, and Median will want the tax rate to jump just above his income, which is between. Secondly, the majority equilibrium is the tax schedule most preferred by the median voter: this schedule will win the votes of Poor and Median against the proposal of Wealthy. A schedule which would place the kink in the tax schedule below the income of the median voter would not muster his support and thus the support of a majority while a schedule that would not tax any voter wealthier than the median would raise less revenue and would be rejected by all voters with incomes equal to or lower than the median. [Unless deadweight losses were really punitive, see Romer, 1975, or voters can be hoodwinked to believe they are.] Finally, if two parties compete to win elections (and conditions discussed above are satisfied), they will converge to the preference of the median voter.

Since decisions are made by the majority rule, one question which appears immediately is why the poor do not take everything from the rich. This is what everyone, Left or Right, had expected — hoped or feared — universal suffrage would lead to. As Ernst Wigforss, the foremost theoretician of the Swedish Social Democracy and the eventual Minister of Finance, said in 1928, "The universal suffrage is incompatible with a society divided into a small class of owners and a large class of unpropertied. Either the rich and the propertied will take away universal suffrage, or the poor, with the help of their right to vote, will procure for themselves a part of the accumulated riches." [Cited in Tingsten, 1973: pp. 274–5; see also Macalay's, 1908, speech on "The Chartists" in 1842 and Marx, 1952: p. 62.] If the electorate consists of *n* persons, the $(n/2 + 1)$ poorest citizens could together pass a proposal which would expropriate the rich. Indeed, we have seen that in the situation analyzed above, the rate of taxation for all incomes higher than the median was unity. Why wouldn't the majority, any majority, expropriate the minority?

Conceivable reasons are many but this literature focuses on dead-weight losses resulting from taxation. Aumann and Kurz [1977: p. 1139] provide the most general formulation when they simply assume that "every agent can, if he wishes, destroy part or all of his endowment."[3] Suppose that individuals supply their endowments in a way that earns incomes $Y(i)$ as long as the tax rate is not larger than some value $t(max)$ but they run away to a non-taxable world of under-ground economy, leisure, or paradise, when their tax rate exceeds $t(max)$ [Romer, 1975]. Now the optimal tax schedule for the median voter and thus the majority equilibrium will be one in which the tax rate jumps to $t(max) < 1$. A higher tax rate would cause everyone subject to taxation to withdraw their endowments from taxable activities and would generate no tax revenue at all. This is the reason cited in this literature to explain why majorities stop short of a completely egali-tarian redistribution.

Deadweight losses provide a topic of discussion several times below but a preliminary comment is needed here. Deadweight losses may occur because labor is withdrawn as the result of taxation or of subsidies to leisure. But they may also occur because households respond to higher taxes by saving less or firms respond by investing less. One interesting consequence of the median voter models is to introduce interdependence of private saving decisions [Bush and MacKay, 1977]. Individuals allocate their income in two steps: first they vote on government programs (whether public goods or pure transfers) and then decide how much of their disposable income to save. The preference of the median voter concerning government programs imposes a budget constraint on the saving decisions of everyone else: everyone has to pay taxes chosen by the median voter before deciding what to do with the remaining income. One could thus expect that the median voter would anticipate the effect of her decision about taxes upon the rate of saving of others and thus upon aggregate income or the tax base. Yet median voter models invariably rely on deadweight losses in the supply of labor and the empirical status of this assumption is doubtful [see Saunders and Klau, 1985: pp. 164–167 for a recent review of evidence]. Indeed, Aumann and Kurz [1977: p. 1157] feel forced to take a somewhat tortured route: in their model dead-weight losses in labor supply constitute a threat which induces a compromise and is, therefore, never fulfilled, so the deadweight losses do not occur. If that is true, then there is no empirical basis on which to estimate the magnitude of these losses.

Note that everyone other than the median voter has reasons to be unhappy with the outcome of majority rule: poor voters would prefer taxes to be higher, rich voters would like to see them lower. Moreover, if the median voter opts for a positive tax, as he typically will, the aggregate income is lower than it would have been if taxes and transfers were zero. Yet any other tax rate would cause someone to lose. In particular, with a lower tax rate, the aggregate income would rise (assuming there are deadweight losses) and the wealthy would pay less in net taxes but the poor would receive less in net benefits. Thus, the median voter majority equilibrium would not be defeated by the unanimity rule: it is Pareto efficient.

What tax schedules will prevail under the assumptions of median voter models? The answer depends, among others, upon restrictions imposed on the admissible tax schedules and the specific assumptions about the deadweight loss function. Most models are based on the assumption that the tax schedule is linear, preferences are quasi-concave, and the tax revenue is totally and equally distributed among individuals. In the simplest model of this kind individuals choose the tax rate that maximizes utility derived from their post-fisc consumption and leisure.[4] If taxes had no effect on aggregate income, then the median voter would choose one of extreme admissible values of the tax rate: zero if her income is equal to or greater than the mean income and one hundred per cent if the median income is less than the mean. Since income distribution is typically skewed to the lower incomes, that is the median is generally lower than the mean, the majority equilibrium would consist of a complete equality of post-fisc incomes. But if taxation causes deadweight losses, the median voter will prefer a tax rate smaller than unity.[5] The general conclusion from models that rely on linear tax schedules is that the winning tax schedule will (1) transfer income from the rich to the poor, (2) provide a negative income tax for the poor, and (3) stop short of perfect equality of post-fisc incomes.[6]

Since the preference of the voter with the median income is decisive under majority rule, median voter models usefully connect information about current conditions to outcomes of political choice. As Romer and Rosenthal [1979: p. 144] remarked, "The great advantage of the median voter paradigm is that it allows one to analyze *social* problems via the preferences of a single *individual*, the pivotal median voter.'' We have seen that the peak preference of the median voter depends on the relation between his income and the mean income. If the distribution of income were perfectly symmetric, that is if the median equalled the mean, the majority would vote for no taxes and no transfers (assuming no special problems are presented by public goods, as this literature tends to assume). As the distribution of pre-fisc income among citizens becomes more inegalitarian, that is as the median falls in relation to the mean, the tax rate preferred by the median voter increases. This result was used by Meltzer and Richard [1981] to explain the growth of government in Western Europe: extensions of franchise and the recent proliferation of voters deriving their income from social security shifted the median income downward in relation to the mean and thus increased the majority equilibrium tax rate. Moreover, Meltzer and Richard note that the median voter model explains the increase of the public debt, since ''The decisive voter has as much incentive to tax the future rich as the current rich.'' [p. 925]

Median voter models have been tested with regard to several policy areas.[7] Pommerehne [1978] found that this model was quite successful in those Swiss municipalities that employed direct democracy. Nevertheless, empirical research generally leads to skeptical conclusions about its validity. Having reviewed several studies of local school expenditures, which provide the most favorable testing grounds for this model, Romer and Rosenthal [1979: p. 144] concluded that they ''fail to indicate that actual expenditures correspond in general to those desired by the median voter.'' [See also Mueller, 1979: pp. 106–109.] Given the severe restrictions on the validity of this model, this conclusion is not surprising.

2.3. The instability of democratic outcomes

The median voter model is both intellectually and normatively attractive. Public policies are explained by citizen preferences and the theory is powerful enough to account for a variety of phenomena, including the historical patterns of state expenditures. Normatively, the median voter model vindicates the democratic ideal: in a democratic polity governments are perfectly responsive and responsible to the wishes of citizens. Unfortunately, this entire intellectual construction is exceedingly fragile.

The conditions under which the median voter model applies, specifically, the conditions under which there exists a majority rule equilibrium, are highly restrictive. It is now well established that no voting procedure will in general produce a transitive ordering of collective preferences. [Arrow, 1951. For reviews of subsequent developments, see Plott, 1976; Mueller, 1979; Schofield, 1978, 1982; Miller, 1983; Suzumura, 1983] Collective choices made by rational individuals at a particular time through any voting procedure are unstable in the sense that the same individual preferences may generate different collective outcomes.

We have seen above that a majority equilibrium exists if there is a proposal which cannot be defeated by majority rule. Such an equilibrium is stable if it results from the voting process regardless of the order in which proposals are paired. When individual preferences are single-peaked and some additional restrictions hold, the majority rule equilibrium exists: this is the central theorem underlying the median voter models. But already with non-linear tax schedules, voter preferences may be such that cycles would appear even in voting on uni-dimensional issues [Foley, 1967]. With more dimensions, it is always possible that even if all voters are rational in the sense that their preferences are transitive (if i prefers X over Y and Y over Z, i prefers X over Z), the collective preference will be intransitive, that is, X will beat Y by the majority rule, Y will beat Z, and Z will beat X. Suppose that individuals vote to decide how much money to raise in taxes, how much of it to spend on public goods, how much on means-tested transfers, and how much on universal grants. In general, there will be no outcome that could not be beaten by some other proposal(s). The core is empty: the core being the set of unbeatable proposals. Moreover, if issues are sufficiently multi-dimensional any outcome is possible, even outcomes that make all people worse off than they were under the status quo without making anyone better off. [McKelvey, 1976.]

These results force a major reinterpretation of the democratic process. A democracy in which citizens are allowed to like whatever they wish, in which everyone's preferences matter for the outcome and no individual's preferences are decisive, and in which outcomes are independent of the sequence in which proposals appear, will not generate a collective preference that could be seen as the unique popular mandate, a reliable expression of the collective will. Indeed, outcomes of voting are unrelated to preferences of voters. Thus, at least in one interpretation [see in particular Riker, 1982], the effect of Arrow's theorem and the subsequent developments was to break the eighteenth century connection between popular sovereignty and collective rationality, understood as transitivity of collective preferences.

Riker [1982] claimed that the impossibility theorems invalidate the interpretation of elections as an expression of popular will and he suggested that we should think of elections as only a negative opportunity to eliminate unwanted rulers. Since elections are not a meaningful mechanism for expressing popular will, they cannot be seen as awarding governments a mandate to pursue any particular policies. Thus Riker called for a minimum government based on negative rights, "liberal" in place of "populist" democracy. Coleman and Ferejohn [1986] pointed out, however, that the impossibility theorems apply with equal force to the choice of governments and the choice of policies: on these grounds there is no reason to prefer liberal over populist democracy. They also joined Shepsle [1979a] in emphasizing that much of the instability of collective choice can be removed by introducing consensual institutional constraints.

The normative issues have traditionally concentrated on Arrow's identification of collective rationality with transitivity or at least a-cyclicity of collective preferences [see Mueller, 1979]. One might consider that any outcome that is reached fairly should be acceptable, even if it could be beaten by the majority rule by some other fair outcome. Moreover, one could argue in the spirit of Dahl [1956] that stable majorities are undesirable since they could oppress minorities: Miller [1983] astutely observed that the paradise lost of the social choice theorist is the paradise regained by the pluralist political theorist. Finally, Schofield [1982, 1985] warned that the chaos of rational politics should not be contrasted with the stable rationality of the market: the edifice of the general equilibrium theory is vulnerable to strategic manipulation by individual agents.

Positive theories of public policy are also profoundly affected by the impossibility results. Miller [1983] went as far as to argue that most voting fluctuations and government turnovers result from the inherent instability of collective choices rather than from changes in the underlying individual preferences. Moreover, even if governments seek to manipulate the economy in order to maximize their electoral support, there is no single policy that would consistently win elections against all alternatives. Thus, Schofield [1985: p. 5] argued that if a government tried to induce electoral business cycles, "there would be no procedure available for it do so in a way which maximized votes, or guaranteed enough votes for re-election."[8] The analytical force of economic theories of democracy is thus almost null if impossibility theorems hold in the real world.

Impossibility theorems rest on several assumptions, each of which has been the subject of extensive debates. The one assumption that is not even explicitly mentioned is that individual preferences are given and remain unchanged during the political process. Viewed from the perspective of economics, the political process consists only of revealing and aggregating exogenously formed individual preferences. Yet it is conceivable that individuals change their preferences as the result of communicating with one another [Sen, 1977; Offe and Wiesenthal, 1980; Elster, 1984; Kolm, 1984]. Unfortunately, we do not have a reasonable description of the way in which preferences change. Riker [1982: p. 122 and p. 128] admitted the possibility that political interactions may modify voter preferences but on unspecified grounds he relegated this possibility to issues that are not politically important. The central issue is whether transitive collective preferences could be induced by a political process in which politicians would deliberately seek to produce an unambiguous and consistent mandate. At this stage, no one seems to know.

3. DEMOCRACY AND EFFICIENCY

3.1. The neo-liberal critique

Even if rational citizens provide an unambiguous, stable expression of their preferences and if governments respond by satisfying the collective preference, any political intervention in the economy is inimical to general welfare. This is the main thrust of one set of views that combines the traditional conservative critique of democracy with a liberal perspective of the economy, specifically, the "theory of regulation" inspired by Stigler and the somewhat distinct theory of "rent seeking society" inspired by Krueger and Tullock.

The central claim of this perspective — I will refer to it as "neo-liberal" — is that the market allocates resources to all uses more efficiently than political institutions. The democratic process is faulty and the state is a source of inefficiency. The state does not even need to do anything for inefficiencies to occur: the very possibility that it might do something is sufficient.

Let us first examine the neo-liberal argument in the version of the "theory of regulation." According to neo-classical economics, a set of complete and competitive markets would allocate resources to private uses in a way that is efficient, exhausts all gains from trade, and would not be altered by a unanimous vote, where these three assertions are equivalent. Such markets would fail, however, to perform efficiently in the presence of various impediments, such as externalities, increasing returns tó scale, transaction costs, etc. [See Bator, 1958, for a list.] Most importantly, markets supply inefficiently goods which are non-rival in consumption, the so-called "public goods." [Samuelson, 1966]. The theory of the state that emerged from neo-classical economics implied that markets should be relied on for providing private goods while the state should provide public goods and should correct other disparities between private and social rates of return by charging Pigovian taxes. As Arrow [1971: p. 137] put it, "when the market fails to achieve an optimal state, society will, to some extent at least, recognize the gap, and nonmarket social institutions will arise attempting to bridge it." [See also Musgrave, 1971.]

Neo-liberals attacked this theory in several ways: (1) by demonstrating that, in the absence of transaction costs, market imperfections can be efficiently dealt with by the market under a suitable distribution of property rights [Coase, 1960]; (2) by pointing out that the notion of market imperfections, including public goods, is unclear and that no theory specifies them ex ante [Stigler, 1975: p. 110]; (3) by remarking that even if the market fails to act efficiently there is no guarantee that the state would do any better [Stigler, 1975, chapter 7; for a classi-fication of "public failures" see Wolf, 1979]; and (4) by claiming that public goods are produced not because they are beneficial to the public which demands them but because they are profitable to the private interests which supply them [again Stigler; Shepsle, 1979b; Shepsle and Weingast, 1984]. The reason the state provides public goods is the same as the reason it does anything else: private self-interest of someone. These arguments serve neo-liberal writers to justify the assumption that competitive markets are efficient, without any distinctions and complications.

Competitive markets would be efficient but now we have a state that intervenes or at least is able to intervene into the economy.[9] The state is referred to here as "the regulator" and not defined or described any further. One characteristic feature of this perspective is that little attention is devoted to political institutions. Politics is seen as basically the same everywhere. Peltzman claims that "there is no need to confine the analysis to democratic societies. As long as suppressing dissent is costly to a dictator, he ought to be sensitive to that popular support for his policies." [1980: p. 221; also Becker 1983: p. 375.][10] The regulator acts in self-interest and again little is said about what the regulator wants. Stigler mentions enrichment as a motive; Hirschleifer in his comment on Peltzman [1976] finds it strange to assume that politicians care about votes while everyone else is assumed to care about money; but in general the story begins one logical step further, with something called "political support." Whatever it is the politicians or bureaucrats may want for themselves, to obtain it they need political support; hence, the common assumption in these theories is that governments maximize support.

Support is something governments buy by transferring income and something groups sell in two forms: direct support (votes in a democracy) and other resources, mainly money, which produce direct support. Transfer of income is understood broadly. Everything governments do results in a transfer of income. Thus Stigler [1975: chapter 8] includes besides direct subsidies of money the control of entry into industries and occupations, controls over substitutes and complements, regulation of prices and fares, etc. Krueger's [1974] list focuses on foreign competition, comprising tariffs, import licenses, and quantitative restrictions and is generalized to include examples such as minimum wages and ceilings on interest rates. Becker [1983: pp. 373–374] classifies transfer instruments into taxes, subsidies, regulations, and others. In general, any government action that makes the equilibrium outcome diverge from the competitive equilibrium constitutes a transfer of income.

Transfers of income necessarily cause inefficiency. What is involved in transfers is not just that someone loses while someone else gains but that the society as a whole suffers net losses. The central concept is "deadweight losses": gains accruing to beneficiaries are always smaller than costs suffered by losers because transfers of income modify behavior.

These losses are of three kinds. First, there are deadweight losses proper. "Every tax affects the tax base": this is the maxim [Peltzman,

1976: 216n]. Taxes reduce demand for labor because they increase labor cost; they decrease investment because they raise costs of capital, and so on. Subsidies are equally inefficient: support for an industry makes its goods cheaper than they should have been in terms of opportunity costs and causes a misallocation of resources. Particularly pernicious are transfers from the rich to the poor: the response of the rich to taxation of profits is to save less, the response of the poor to transfers is to work less, and the deadweight losses are compounded. The "empirical" estimates of the cost of deadweight losses are often astronomical. [I put "empirical" in quotation marks because the procedure is often to assume some elasticities and simulate, rather than estimate. See Browning and Johnson, 1984; Stuart, 1984; Ballard, Shoven, and Whalley, 1985.]

Besides these standard reasons, two other sources of inefficiency are highlighted by the theory of "rent seeking society." [Tollison, 1982, provides a summary; Buchanan, Tollison, and Tullock, 1980, is a collection of recent work.] These are rents dissipated by governments and the resources wasted in trying to influence the government to provide rents. We return to these categories below.

Since government intervention is always inefficient, how does it happen that governments do exist, regulate, tax, subsidize, impose barriers to entry, etc.? Presumably at least in a democracy, self-interested, rational citizens would vote against every kind of government intervention. But this is not the case. The reason is that the democratic process is necessarily faulty and citizens are rationally ignorant and manipulable. Since this is the core of the theory, let us stay closer to texts.

The democratic process is inherently "gross or filtered or noisy." [Stigler, 1975: p. 126]. Voting can take place only infrequently; votes must decide all kinds of issues simultaneously; the alternatives facing them can be formulated only crudely. Moreover, in a democracy everyone can vote, "not simply those who are directly concerned with a decision" [ibidem: p. 124]. Votes affect decisions on issues about which the particular voter may care little or not at all. And since benefits of government interventions tend to be concentrated while their costs are diffuse, individuals have few incentives to learn about all issues on which they vote. [Downs, 1957; Becker, 1958; Stigler, 1975]. They are ignorant rationally but ignorant nevertheless. "The political decision process," Stigler [1975: p. 124] observes, "cannot exclude the uninterested voter. . . . Hence, the political process does not allow participation in proportion to interest and knowledge." Moreover, this balance between costs and benefits of information implies that voters can be manipulated by being fed information and persuasion by interested parties [Peltzman, 1976; Becker, 1983]. This is why the support offered by particular groups in exchange for rents includes not only votes but resources with which to produce votes (money, organization, etc.) and this is why individual voters are ultimately not sovereign. "I believe," Becker [1983: p. 392] declares, "that voter preferences are frequently not a crucial *independent* force in political behavior."

Contrast the democratic process with the market. In the market no one is compelled to decide matters of no personal interest to him or her. Stigler's example merits attention: "In a private market, the non-traveler never votes on rail versus plane travel, while the huge shipper casts many votes each day." [1975: p. 124] In the market decisions are made all the time and they are discriminating: if I want to buy olives, I compare prices of olives and buy olives; I am not forced to buy anything else. In the market information is cheap and it flows continuously: every time I go to a store I find what the current price of olives is. Thus Becker notes [1983: p. 392] that "the average person knows far more about supermarket prices or the performance of cars than about import quotas or public wages." As a result, Stigler [1975: p. 126] concludes, "The expressions of preferences in voting will be less precise than the expressions of preferences in the marketplace because many uninformed people will be voting and affecting the decision."

The market is just a superior mechanism for revealing sovereign preferences. The traditional liberal reason is emphasized by Tollison [1982: p. 589]: "The market is a proprietary setting where individuals bear the consequences of their actions in the form of changes in their net wealth. The political setting is a non-proprietary setting where individual agents do not always feel the full benefit and cost of their decisions." And the conclusion [1982: p. 594] follows: "The point of this discussion is that political competition under one man-one vote conditions does not lead to efficient outcomes in the same sense that such outcomes are produced by competition in private markets." Or, as Burke wrote about the distribution of income through taxation, is it "better to leave all dealing, in which there is no force or fraud, collision or combination, entirely to the persons mutually concerned in the matter contracted for; or to put the contract in the hands of those, who can have none, or a very remote interest in it, and little or no knowledge of the subject." [1984: p. 62] Indeed, Burke's *Thoughts and Details on Scarcity*, written in 1795, presage most arguments discussed above, including even the deadweight losses.

3.2. Is democracy inefficient?

Two technical points — one empirical and one conceptual — are important in evaluating the neo-liberal arguments. The empirical issue concerns deadweight losses: whether these are indeed prevalent and unavoidable.[11] This issue will not be discussed here; we return to one crucial aspect below, in the discussion of private property. The conceptual issue concerns the concept of efficiency, understood as Pareto optimality.

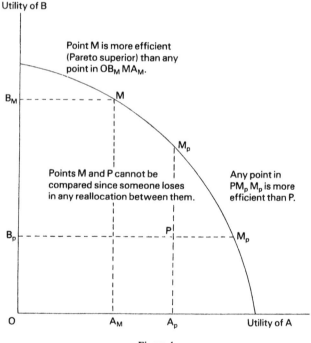

Figure 1

In the neo-liberal view government intervention always introduces inefficiency. The assumption must be that the society first reaches some point which is efficient, that is, which lies at the Pareto frontier, and then enters the government, which causes deadweight losses to occur and pushes the allocation of resources to a point inferior to the original one. But the general thesis is not warranted, for several reasons.

First, not all allocations of resources can be compared in the technical language of efficiency. [For a clarification of these issues and a similar critique see Coleman, 1982 a and b] Suppose the market (in which some agents vote their preferences several times a day while others never do) allocates resources in a way M, which is efficient. Suppose the democratic system (in which everyone has one vote, even poor people) allocates resources in a way P. Is it always true that P is less efficient then M? The answer is "no": several possible allocations M and P cannot be compared with regard to efficiency. Point M may lie on a possibility frontier that is farther out than point P but moving from P to M would make someone worse off: hence M is not Pareto superior to P.[12] Unless there exists an alternative which would make everyone better or equally well off, a policy is not inefficient.

Secondly, to say that a policy causes deadweight loss is to assert that it reduces national income but not that it necessarily reduces social welfare. Government actions typically hurt some people and benefit others. That aggregate losses of income exceed aggregate gains is not relevant unless utility is measured by money.[13] Thus, even if it were true that government interventions necessarily decrease aggregate income, the inferences from losses of income to those of welfare cannot be sustained.

Finally, the model proposed by Peltzman [1976] and elaborated by Becker [1976, 1983] implies in fact that the political allocation must be Pareto efficient. Suppose it were not. Then, by definition, there would exist some alternative policy (including non-intervention) which would make at least one person better off and none worse off. In Figure 1, every point on the utility possibility frontier between Mp and Mp is Pareto superior to P and would produce greater political support than P. If any such point were economically feasible, P would never be chosen by a support-maximizing politician. Hence, whatever is the choice of a support-maximizing politician, it must lie on the utility possibility frontier.[14]

To conclude, the technical language is not correctly used by neo-liberal writers who must be relying on an implicit and prior assumption that allocations resulting from the democratic process are inferior to market solutions on grounds other than efficiency. The proposition that every government intervention is a source of inefficiency cannot be sustained within the language of economic theory.

While the views discussed above emphasize the alleged inefficiency of policy outcomes, another perspective focuses on the waste involved in the political process. The neo-liberal view of the political process becomes most apparent in the theory of "rent seeking society." [Krueger, 1974, provided a still reasonable version of this theory.] In this account, the government is a source of potential rents. Since there are rents to be gained, economic agents compete to obtain them. For example, if rents are created by quantitative restrictions on imports and if import licenses are distributed in proportion to company size, companies increase their size to compete for the licenses. Efficiency thus suffers for two reasons: the standard reason, namely, protection, and the additional reason, namely, the waste involved in inefficiently large companies.

This story assumes a general form of "theory of society" in the writings of Buchanan, Tollison, and Tullock [1980] and their colla-borators. Government intervention generates rents: this is a waste of consumer surplus. If governments themselves appropriate the rents, they are likely to dissipate them through unproductive activities [see in particular Tullock's response to Bhagwati]. On top of all this, everyone wastes resources trying to influence the government. The last point constitutes the specific focus of this argument. Suppose that two industries wine and dine government officials, one lobbying for and the other against a tariff and that at the end the government decides not to introduce this tariff [Young, 1982]. Efficiency does not suffer from government intervention: the government has not intervened. Yet resources were wasted on trying to influence the government: the very ability of the government to intervene is a cause of waste. Even if the government were eventually to introduce a tariff and cause inefficiency in this way, resources might have been saved if the decision was made without any influence. What should governments do then? Answer: we would be better off if they just did without the influence whatever they would have done under the influence. And how are they to know what? They should listen to economists.[15] The sublime logic of this theory is captured by Dixit and Grossman [1984], who point out that many resources would be saved if places in heaven were awarded deus ex machina, without anyone having to go through the process.

The political process is exactly what constitutes waste in this perspective. This theory takes the neo-classical method to its ultimate conclusion: preferences of individuals are exogenous and fixed and equilibrium is reached instantaneously. Hence, there is neither need nor place for any kind of a process: preferences will not be altered and the outcome is known directly from preferences and constraints. At least in the "theory of regulation," the "Chicago" version of neo-liberalism, political process is ultimately found inferior to the market because of its imperfections. In the "theory of rent seeking society," the "Virginia" version, there is no place for politics: politics is just a waste.

Thus, the conclusions of the neo-liberal perspective are based on a prior preference for the market and on a bias due to the method of reasoning. The ideological preference for private property, which is normally expressed by phrases about "interest" and "responsibility," leads neo-liberal writers not only to reject all notions that an allocation of resources can be evaluated by distributional criteria but also to forward a claim that cannot be fully sustained by the assumptions of the theory, namely, that allocations of resources resulting from preferences of citizens revealed through the democratic process are necessarily less efficient than market solutions. The methodological bias — that preferences are fixed and adjustment to equilibrium is instantaneous — leads to a neglect or outright rejection of the democratic process.

4. OPEN ISSUES

Four assumptions of economic theories of democracy seem particularly questionable: (1) that individual preferences are fixed, (2) that politicians compete for political support, (3) that individuals are directly represented in the political process, and (4) that, once elected, governments are perfect agents of their constituencies.

4.1. Preferences

The first question is to what extent and how individual preferences change through the political process. Is politics only an arena, where actors with externally given interests fight to promote them, or an *agora*, where individuals discover through discursive interactions what their collective identities and thus their interests are? Most of sociology, from Durkheim to Gramsci to Parsons, insists that identity formation is a continuing social process: conceptions of interests as well as images of the constraining reality are generated continually as the result of social interactions. [For a recent critique of economic theories based on this position see Pizzorno, 1985.] But the relevant issue is narrower: not whether individual preferences ever change as the result of some social processes but whether they change endogenously through political interactions. The question is whether voters are persuaded to dislike inflation just by the promises of politicians to eradicate it; whether they are taught by political parties that government deficits are the cause of inflation, etc.

The answer to such questions is undoubtedly positive: preferences of individuals are altered in the political process. We have seen that the Chicago school maintains that individual preferences are indeed manipulated by groups which spend money and organizational resources to inform and persuade voters. " 'Preferences'," Becker puts the word in quotation marks, "can be manipulated and created through the information and misinformation provided by interested pressure groups. . . ." "Pressure groups can 'purchase' favorable votes with lobbying and other political activities. . . ." [1983: p. 392] Needless to say, this conception of individual preferences is shared with only slight changes of language by left-wing critics of capitalist democracies. Citizens in a democracy are not sovereign because they are ideologically dominated by the bourgeoisie and manipulated by privately owned mass media: this is a persistent left-wing theme. [Miliband, 1969; Anderson, 1977]

If individual preferences are continually transformed through the political process, economic theories of democracy suffer two major consequences. Models of party competition cannot be based on the assumption that the distribution of preferences, "the public opinion," is something given independently to the competing parties. This distribution is an effect, a contingent outcome of, among others, competition among parties. [For a theoretical elaboration of this process see Gramsci, 1971. Przeworski and Sprague, 1986, showed that electoral strategies of European socialist parties determine whether workers vote on the basis of class.] Thus Downsian models of party competition are fundamentally misspecified. Political parties do not simply adjust their proposals to the pre-existing "public opinion"; they shape this opinion. If citizen preferences were fixed exogenously, there would be no reason for parties to do anything but instantaneously jump to the equilibrium: the paradox of Downs' theory is not only that individuals vote but also that parties compete. Invocations of Schumpeter as the intellectual father of the "economic theory of democracy" are misdirected. Schumpeter did consider democracy as a competition among elites seeking to conquer political power but he saw the political process as one of persuasion: "What we are confronted with in the analysis of political processes," he insisted, "is largely not a genuine but a manufactured will . . . . the will of the people is the product and not the motive power of the political process." [1975: p. 263, also 258, 270] The Downsian model simplified this conception of democratic competition and deprived it of explanatory power.

The implications of endogenous preference formation for the existence and the stability of majority rule equilibrium have already been discussed. The assumption of fixed exogenous preferences may or may not accurately characterize contemporary politics but arguments derived from this assumption certainly do not suffice as a critique of the concept of popular democracy as it was elaborated during the eighteenth century and eventually used to provide the ideological foundations for the modern representative institutions. Whether in Rousseau's conception of general will [Keohane, 1980, chapter 15] or the American revolutionary thought between 1776 and 1787 [Wood, 1969], individual preferences were thought to be transformed in the pursuit of common interest. And the common interest was not the sum of whatever interests individuals would have pursued prior to the political interaction, for politics, as Wood put it, "was conceived to be not the reconciling but the transcending of the different interests of the society in the search for the single common good. . . ." [1969: pp. 57–58] Intransitivity of collective preferences would furnish a devastating critique of "populist" conceptions of democracy if it were shown either that citizens are in fact not "virtuous," that is, they are unwilling to modify preferences when faced with the knowledge of the resulting collective irrationalities, or if intransitivities continue to occur even if citizens are full of republican virtue. Either of these assertions may be true but thus far they have not shown to be. In spite of Riker's [1982] premature closure, the full implications of

Arrow's theorem for the conceptions of democracy are yet to be explored.

4.2. Political competition

The treatment of political competition is a particularly weak aspect of economic theories of democracy. The assumption that politicians care only about political support, specifically votes under democracy, and that they are willing to take any position and enter any coalition to win elections is implausible. There is something strange about a theory which assumes that people derive utility from consumption and leisure unless and until they become politicians, in which case their only source of satisfaction are votes. That politicians prefer to be popular rather than not is certain, but the autonomous importance of power in their utility functions is perhaps the grand unresolved issue of political science. The paradoxical nature of this assumption is demonstrated by the conclusion that politicians are not voters in this theory: voters care about policies but politicians have no such preferences. What would constitute evidence about the motivations of politicians is not easy to define, for the prior question is under what constraints parties maximize votes. The distribution of citizen preferences is not the only constraint parties face: party leaders have to worry about mobilizing activists, about satisfying party bureaucrats, sometimes about not offending related organizations, such as the trade unions or churches, and so forth. This is why Wittman's [1983] evidence that party leaders are not solely vote-oriented is unpersuasive one way or another.

Secondly, there is a real question to what extent parties do compete. Crain [1977] pointed out that under the single member system incumbents do not compete with each other: they only compete against challengers. [Wittman, 1973, thought that parties which maximize votes do compete.] Thus incumbents have powerful incentives to restrict competition. After all, the most protected industry in the United States is electoral politics: according to Rae [1967], historically a party had to obtain about 10 per cent of the total vote to win the first seat in the House of Representatives.

Finally, the Hotelling–Downs model of party competition yields the majority equilibrium at best for two parties. Greenberg and Weber [1985] have succeeded only recently to confirm Downs' conjecture that, under the same restricted conditions concerning voter preferences, the competition for votes results in an equilibrium also when there are more parties. But since the winners in a multi-party system need not constitute a majority, a coalition theory is required additionally before electoral competition can be related to policy outcomes. Yet coalition theories remain unsatisfactory. Riker's [1962] theory of minimal winning coalitions met with objections, on the one hand, from economists who argued that pay-offs are continuously associated with the size of electoral coalitions [Stigler, 1972] and, on the other hand, from political scientists, who insisted that ideological factors prevent parties from forming just any coalitions. Yet the empirical support for coalition theories, including Axelrod's [1970] "minimum connected winning coalition," is weak [Wright and Goldberg, 1985].

In conclusion, there are no good reasons to believe that, save for exceptional circumstances assumed by the Hotelling–Downs theorem, competition among politicians will lead them to the majority rule equilibrium even if one exists. The very concepts of political competition and of support market are based on an analogy that falls short of providing a workable model.

4.3. Representation of interests

The economic theory of democracy admits two classes of actors: individuals and (teams of) politicians, one of which becomes the government. The Chicago school introduces again some realism by theorizing about pressure groups which buy government policies and sell political support. Even here, however, groups are nothing but ephemeral coalitions of individuals, any coalition is likely, and the exchange market consists of such groups and governments. As Becker [1983: p. 388] puts it, "In all societies virtually an unlimited number of pressure groups could form a lobby for political aid to their members, categorized by occupation, industry, income, sex, age, height, consumption, and other characteristics." Without going to the other extreme — that there are always two and only two political actors and these are classes [see the Manley–Dahl–Lindblom debate, 1983] — it is apparent that forms of representation of interests are not limited to ephemeral interest groups and that many important decisions in countries normally considered as democracies do not pass through electoral politics at all.

Indeed, even in democratic societies, the so-called "voluntary associations" normally involve an element of compulsion. As Stepan [1978: p. 15] pointed out, "for most societies throughout most of history, interest groups have not been at liberty to 'freely combine'." Schmitter [1974, 1977] emphasized the importance of the "neo-corporatist" system of representation of interests. In this system, a handful of organizations, principally business associations and labor unions, enjoy a virtual and at times legal monopoly of representing functionally defined interests. This monopoly endows these associations with coercive powers over the members and gives them the status of what Schmitter and Streeck [1981] eventually called "private government." An enormous, primarily descriptive, literature grew around this theme. [See Cawson and Ballard, 1984, for the bibliography.]

Two central questions remain, however, open. The first concerns the micro-foundations of the corporatist system of representation. In his original article, Schmitter gave a functionalist explanation of the origins of corporatism: it was necessary for the development of capitalism [also Strinati, 1979]. Recently, he claimed that the origins of corporatism can be found neither in the functional requirements of capitalism nor in the interests of the individual members of the corporatist association but in the collusion between leaders of these associations and government bureaucrats [1986]. Unfortunately, this theory is too sketchy to be persuasive. Wallerstein [1984] developed a model that explains the cross-national variations in union centralization — the critical feature of corporatist systems — but he began the analysis with already existing unions rather than with individual workers. [For alternative formulations of strategic problems of workers, see Schwerin, 1982; Streeck, 1984; Offe, 1985.] Bowman [1982, 1985] studied micro-foundations of trade associations, with the general conclusion that such arrangements should be highly unstable. The question of whose interests are served by the corporatist system remains highly controversial. [Panitch, 1980]

The second question concerns the relation between the electoral ("parliamentary" in the European terminology) and the corporatist systems. In the view of Schmitter [1983], Schwerin [1982], Offe [1984] and several others, the corporatist system displaced representation through political parties and parliaments and, given that the access to the corporatist system is limited and the associations wield monopoly power, corporatism develops at the expense of and as a threat to democracy. Lembruch [1982] and Panitch [1981], however, argued that the corporatist system supplements rather than displaces parliamentary institutions: those countries where corporatist arrangements are strong are those in which the functional scope of state activities is most extensive. This seems like a straightforward empirical issue but somehow there is no consensus.

Whatever theoretical issues remain open, neo-corporatist institutions are obviously important in the life of several Western European countries, particularly Austria, Sweden, Norway, and Switzerland, and to a lesser extent Germany, Denmark, Netherlands, Belgium, and Finland. The crucial aspect of corporatist associations is that they internalize a large part of the social costs of their actions. Thus a highly centralized union federation must be concerned about inflationary consequences of its wage demands while a particular union within a fragmented system can expect to bear only a small part of such costs. Numerous empirical studies demonstrate that variously measured "corporatism" is a good predictor of the behavior of labor unions, of the dynamics of wages, of economic performance and of government spending. [Bruno and Sachs, 1985; Cameron, 1984; Castles, 1987; Crouch, 1985; Garrett and Lange, 1988; Hicks, 1988; Lange, 1984b; Lange and Garrett, 1985; Marks, 1986; McCallum, 1987; Schmidt, 1982; Schott, 1984; Wilensky, 1981] Although to my knowledge no one has confronted directly the predictions that result from the median voter model with those postulated by the theory of corporatism, the strength of neo-corporatist institutions seems to be far more successful in explaining government policies and their economic consequences.

4.4. State autonomy

Finally, not only economic theories of democracy but all theories which see government decisions as responses to external demands fail to consider that governments may have the institutional capacity and state managers may have the will to act independently of outside influences. Instead of responding to demands, the state may supply policies autonomously, whether in the self-interest of state managers or in the interest of the public as interpreted by state managers. Several theories, derived from different theoretical assumptions and applied to different historical contexts, maintain that state policies are better understood by considering the factors that determine their supply. These theories are reviewed below.

Part II: The Rule of the State

1. INTRODUCTION

One question left open by economic theories of democracy is why would politicians ever bother to seek popular support. Why would they not seek instead to liberate themselves from dependence on the support by anyone else? If state managers have values and interests of their own, would they not impose them on the society? A large body of political theory maintains that this is precisely what politicians and bureaucrats always try to do and that they are often successful. State managers perennially struggle to escape external control and to establish their own rule. When they are successful, the result is state autonomy. To use Marx's imagery, the state becomes the "master" rather than the "servant" of society.

Several theories explain policies of governments by preferences of state managers and characteristics of state institutions. According to these theories, state managers have goals of their own and under some institutional and political conditions they are able to pursue success-fully policies oriented to fulfill these goals.

The goals of state managers may reflect their individual self-interest, institutional interests of the state, or some conception of the common good. "Property rights" theories of the state assume that rulers pursue their own interests. "Organic" theories, beginning with Aristotle, see the state as a morally motivated actor, seeking to coordinate individual goals and actions on behalf of some values conceptualized as "common good," "public interest," and the like. [See Stepan, 1978, for a summary of such theories.] In either case, however, the state is autonomous since state managers — collectively "the state" — do not act on behalf of any outsiders.

Four questions organize this perspective: (1) How frequently and to what extent are states autonomous? (2) What conditions promote autonomy? (3) What are the consequences of different forms of state for government policies? (4) How do bureaucrats and politicians manage to become autonomous under democratic conditions?

Since the very concept of autonomy remains a muddle, some terminological preliminaries must be cleared before substantive questions can be discussed. This is done in Section 2. The subject of Section 3 are theories, mostly of marxist inspiration, which explain the origins of state autonomy. Section 4 offers an analysis, based on the property rights approach, of the consequences of different forms of state for public policy. The possibility that the state would be autonomous under democracy is examined in Section 5, first with regard to the bureaucracy and then more generally.

2. TERMINOLOGICAL PRELIMINARIES

The state is autonomous when state managers have the institutional capacity to choose their own goals and to realize them in the face of conflicting interests. Skocpol's definition is representative: "States conceived as organizations claiming control over territories and people may formulate and pursue goals that are not simply reflective of the demands or interests of social groups, classes, or society. This is what is usually meant by 'state autonomy'." [1985: p. 9]

Terminological difficulties arise because assertions of autonomy answer two distinct questions: Are state managers able to choose the goals of state activity? Can they realize their goals, however these are chosen? For example, Krasner [1984: p. 224] poses the question of autonomy by asking whether the state can "formulate and implement its preferences?" Yet the capacity to formulate and to implement need not go together, at least for two reasons.

(1) State managers may have institutional capacity to choose goals of their own yet they may be systematically barred from pursuing some courses of action and, thus, they may be unable to generate some outcomes.

One limitation arises from the structure of the economy. The freedom of action which is guaranteed to private economic actors under capitalism may render some forms of state intervention structurally impossible. Under capitalism, private ownership of one's own labor capacity and of capital impose definite limits on state functions. Private ownership of capital implies that the state cannot mandate investment; private ownership of the capacity to work prevents the state from commanding labor. (Note that the exceptional periods when governments used such policies are referred to as "war socialism.")

Given these structural limitations, governments must rely in economic interventions on incentives rather than commands. Several writers have used the concept of "complementarity": only those state interventions can be effective which are compatible with goals of those affected by the particular policy. Offe's analysis is particularly cogent: "the political system can only make offers to external, autonomous bodies responsible for decisions: either these offers are not accepted, thus making the attempts at direction in vain, or the offers are so attractive in order to be accepted that the political direction for its part loses its autonomy because it has to internalize the aims of the system to be directed." [1974: p. 175]

Finally, an important limitation on state actions is institutional. States constitute complex organizations [Padgett, 1981]. Their organizational structure enables certain policies and prevents others. Collecting income taxes, for example, requires an enormous information system; state managers cannot simply decide to institute income tax. As Evans and Rueschemeyer emphasize, "An effective bureaucratic machinery is the key to the state's capacity to intervene." [1985: p. 51] Moreover, institutional factors, such as independence of central monetary authorities from the executive, predispose states to particular policy styles. As a result, as Hall [1984] demonstrated, economic policies differ more between countries than between governments within each country. [In the marxist literature, Hirsch, 1978, emphasized the limitations of state interventionism due to its structure.]

(2) Once the state acquires the capacity to intervene into the economy, economic actors have incentives to seek control over the state. As Rueschemeyer and Evans [1985: p. 69] observed, "Increased penetration of civil society by the state activates political responses and increases the likelihood that societal interests will attempt to invade and divide the state." The result is that as the capacity of the state to implement its preferences increases, its capacity to formulate them independently declines.

This is the often told story of Keynesianism. [Skidelsky, 1977 and

1979] Indeed, one can provide an account of the role of the state regarding the economy about which Stigler [1975] and Habermas [1975] would agree. Until the Great Depression the state only assured the operation of the market but did not intervene. There was thus no reason for private interests to seek control over the state. Then came the Keynesian revolution: the state acquired the capacity to manage the economy. But as the result of its newly acquired powers, it soon lost the ability to resist pressures from private groups which now had good reasons to seek influence over the state. Permeated by private interests, the state began to generate massive inefficiencies as it responded to conflicting pressures, in particular for accumulation and legitimation. By that time marxists concluded that a failure of reproduction is possible: a diagnosis shared by neo-liberals, who responded with a revolution against the state.

Whether this historical account is accurate, the moral of the story is that states become vulnerable to outside influences precisely when they become effective in transforming the economy. Hence, they can be either autonomous in choosing goals and impotent in realizing them or effective in intervening but vulnerable to private interests.

To conclude, the ability of state managers to choose their objectives should be kept analytically distinct from the capacity of state institutions to realize these objectives. The state is "autonomous" when it formulates its own goals and realizes them in the face of opposition. It is "instrumental" when it acts effectively as an agent of some external interests. It is irrelevant when it cannot do much, whether in pursuit of its own objectives or anyone else's.

This is why the notion of "strong state" continues to be a source of confusion when it juxtaposes the "weakest state . . . that is completely permeated by pressure groups" to "one that is able to remake the society and culture in which it exists — that is, to change economic institutions, values, and patterns of interaction among private groups" [Krasner, 1978: p. 56]. A state completely permeated by pressure groups may be highly effective in changing economic institutions, values, and patterns of interaction; indeed, the "strongest" state, if this word has any meaning, is probably one that uses organized violence on behalf of economically dominant interests and not a state that ventures against them.

3. THE ORIGINS OF STATE AUTONOMY

3.1. The "relative autonomy" approach

Given the terminological difficulties, it is perhaps not surprising that radically conflicting empirical claims are made regarding relations between states and societies. For Bentley [1908], Truman [1951], Easton [1965], and their pluralist followers, no state is ever independent. Bentley did not flinch from confronting the extreme case: "When we take such an agency of government as a despotic ruler, we cannot possibly advance to an understanding of him except in term of the group activities of his society which are most directly represented through him. Always and everywhere our study must be a study of the interests that work through government; otherwise we have not got down to the fact." [pp. 270-271] The state is always and everywhere an expression of society: it is but a channel for exercising influence. In fact, to be truthful to the pluralist terminology we should have avoided the term "state." In Easton's view, all we have is a system which transforms outside influences into authoritative decisions, without any specific effect of its own.

Bentley's claim is a haunting one, as we often demonstrate in the intuitive search for social bases of apparently autonomous dictatorships. But even if we accept the premise that normally the state acts as an agent of some groups external to it, there may exist some conditions under which no social group could or would want to establish its control over the state. Under such conditions the state becomes "autonomous."

The concept of "autonomy" originates from theories, principally of marxist inspiration, which have the following structure. If some conditions are true of civil society, specifically, if the economically dominant class is capable of organizing itself politically and if it does not face equally powerful opponents, then the dominant class conquers the state and rules directly. If either of these conditions is violated, then the state becomes independent from the society. When the state is instrumental, interests of the economically dominant class dictate what the state does. When the state is autonomous, its policies do not systematically reflect interests of the dominant class. But the very relation between the state and the society — whether under particular historical conditions the state is autonomous or instrumental — is explained by class relations. Hence, even if state policies cannot be reduced to social conditions, the autonomy of the state can be [Laclau, 1977, chapter 2]. As Elster [1985: pp. 405–6] put it, state autonomy "may be explained by the fact that it is useful for the economically dominant class — or it may be allowed by the fact that there is no single dominant class." Autonomy is thus always "relative" in the sense that the state becomes autonomous only under certain conditions of society.[16]

The substance of these theories is summarized below; at this moment their structure needs further elaboration. As Elster [1985: p. 405] notes, "the autonomy is defined negatively, as the absence of class explanation." The negative language indeed dominates definitions of autonomy: Trimberger, to cite one more example, sees the state apparatus as autonomous when state managers "(1) are not recruited from the dominant landed, commercial, or industrial classes; and (2) they do not form close personal and economic ties with those classes after their elevation to high office" [1978: p. 4].

But the concept of autonomy does not simply deny that the state acts on behalf of some external principle. Theories of state autonomy necessarily entail the counterfactual claim that the state could be an instrument of some specific outsider. Assertions that the state is autonomous with regard to a particular group are of interest only when a plausible presumption is established that this group could, under specifiable conditions, control the state. The observation that in the United States today state institutions are autonomous with regard to children seems less interesting that a suggestion that they are auto-nomous with regard to the electorate. The long-standing interest in state autonomy among marxists is due to the fact that marxist theory viewed periods when the state is autonomous as exceptional: under normal capitalist circumstances the state was expected to function in the interest of the bourgeoisie. The assertions that bureaucrats and politicians act in their self-interest under democracy derive their shock value from the theory which expects them to act as perfect agents of the electorate. In all such cases the observation that the state is autonomous is a source of puzzlement because of a causal model which predicts that the state would act as a perfect agent of some external principle.

Moreover, the concept of autonomy is specific to a referent. The state may be independent from one group and be a perfect agent of another. In the interpretation of Chandra [1980], the colonial state was free from control by the local bourgeoisie but remained a tool of foreign capital. The Keynesian state may have been autonomous from the bourgeoisie but was responsive to a coalition between unions and firms [Przeworski and Wallerstein, 1982]. Even more complex possibilities have been entertained: the state may be independent from the particularistic interests of firms and yet act as a perfect agent of the collective interest of capital. [This is the essence of Poulantzas', 1973, theory.] Thus assertions that the state is autonomous *tout court* are equivalent to the proposition that it is independent from all the eventual principals. Note that Skocpol, cited above, is forced to provide their complete list: a state is autonomous when its goals and policies "are not simply reflective of . . . social groups, classes, or society."[17]

Thus, the concept of autonomy has place only in the context of theories which demonstrate that some specific groups, organizations, or coalitions thereof under some specifiable circumstances could control the state. "Autonomy" is a useful instrument of analysis when it denotes one among possible historical situations.

3.2. The origins of autonomy

According to Marx, the state would be an instrument of the capitalist class whenever this class could organize itself politically and whenever it did not face an equally powerful opponent in other classes. Marx seems to have thought that these conditions would normally prevail under capitalism and he thus treated the instances when the state had become autonomous as exceptional. The perception of the autonomous state as exceptional was shared by Gramsci [1971] as well as several marxist interpreters of fascism [Thalheimer, 1979 (1930); see Adler, 1979]. Recent marxists, however, from Poulantzas [1973] to Elster [1985], see state autonomy as the prevalent relation between political institutions and the capitalist economy.

How does the state become autonomous? As noted above, marxist theories seek an answer to this question in class relations. The manner in which class relations promote state autonomy has been the subject of two distinct theories.

3.2.1 Abdication/abstention theory   In this theory the bourgeoisie is able to rule directly but finds it in the best interest not to do so. In England and Prussia the bourgeoisie "abstained" from taking power and allowed the aristocracy to govern. In France, where the bourgeoisie ruled directly until 1848 and where it continued to struggle for power until 1850, it "abdicated." The "abdication" theory was explicitly put forward by Marx in his writings on France between 1848 and 1851 [1934, 1952] and Stepan [1985: p. 319] refers to it as the standard marxist account of state autonomy. The common structure of explanations in terms of "abdication" and "abstention" was recently reconstructed by Elster [1985].

The assumption here is that the bourgeoisie has the economic importance and the organizational capacity necessary to conquer and to wield state power. But, on the one hand, the cost of struggling for and eventually exercising political power is high for individual capitalists, who want only "to exploit the other classes and to enjoy undisturbed property, family, religion and order. . . ." [Marx, 1934: p. 55] The experience of universal suffrage proved to the bourgeoisie that "the struggle to maintain its *public* interests, its own *class interests*, its *political power*, only troubled and upset it, as it was a disturbance of private business" [p. 89]. On the other hand, the individual capitalists expect they will be able to successfully pursue their private affairs under the protection of the dictatorship. Thus the bourgeoisie abdicates from the struggle for political power and the state becomes autonomous. In Marx's [p. 91] words, the "extra-parliamentary mass of the bourgeoisie . . . invited Bonaparte to suppress and annihilate its speaking and writing section, its politicians and its *literati*, its platform and its press, in order that it might then be able to pursue its private affairs with the full confidence in the protection of a strong and unrestricted government."[18] As Elster argues [1985: p. 411], "There is an explanatory connection: the bourgeoisie abdicate from power (France) or abstain from taking it (England, Germany) because they perceive that their interests are better served if they remain outside politics."

Obviously, the question to be asked of this theory is whether the individual bourgeois are in fact making a good deal when they opt for the protection of a strong and unrestricted government? Will their interests be indeed better served if they give up the struggle for political power? Marx seems to have taken for granted that the Bonapartist regime would not hurt the French bourgeoisie and marxists ever since have been equally ready to assume that no autonomous state could or would hurt the interests of the abdicating or abstaining bourgeoisie.

The assumption, made explicit by Poulantzas [1973] and Block [1977] is that even if the state is not guided by interests of the capitalist class as its objective, in a capitalist economy any state is still constrained by bourgeois interests to the point that no state can threaten capitalism. The state depends on capital for the realization of its goals, whatever they are; hence the bourgeoisie is protected regardless who rules.

The question of structural dependence of states on capital is the subject of the following section. At this moment it suffices to point out that there are quite a few historical instances in which autonomous states turned against the bourgeoisie, whether in the self-interest of generals or for other reasons. Just during the past 20 years in Latin America, this has been the experience of Brazil, where the military-created state sector successfully competes with private firms, of Chile where the state under Pinochet "turned a deaf ear to the national bourgeoisie," [Stepan, 1985: p. 324], of Argentina under Martinęz de Hoz whose policies forced out of business almost one half of firms, of Peru and Ecuador where technocrats decided they knew better what is best for their countries than local capitalist [Conaghan, 1985]. Perhaps the destruction of inefficient local firms by these bureaucratic-authoritarian regimes has been salutary for the development of capitalism but the capitalists, who are said to abdicate from political power in their self-interest, care not about capitalism in general but about continuing as capitalists themselves. And why would an autonomous state promote or even protect interests of the bourgeoisie, even more specifically, of those firms whose owners or managers throw their fates at the mercy of generals? The abdication/abstention theory is not persuasive unless capitalists have good reasons to trust that the autonomous state would protect their interests and, as Elster put it, "Marx never succeeded in proving that the state in a capitalist state must be a capitalist state" [1985: p. 421].

3.2.2. The weak bourgeoisie theory   The standard account of state autonomy in the less developed countries begins with the observation that the bourgeoisie there does not have the faculties which it possessed in the "classical case" of Western Europe. The bourgeoisie in the less developed countries is "weak" because capitalistically organized production is less important economically, because it is divided along sectoral lines [Przeworski, 1981], because it depends on links with foreign capital [Frank, 1979], because it does not have the requisite organizational or ideological resources or skills [Cardoso, 1971]. The weak bourgeoisie is unable to organize or to conquer the state, thus leaving a space for state autonomy. The state becomes autonomous by default of the bourgeoisie.

To argue that the state is autonomous because the bourgeoisie is weak entails the assumption that it would have not been autonomous had the bourgeoisie been strong: otherwise the theory would have no causal force. To validate this assumption, writers in this tradition draw contrasts between the Third World and "the classical case of Western Europe," claiming that (1) in Europe the bourgeoisie built the state and ruled directly while in the periphery the state has been autonomous with regard to the local classes and (2) in Europe the state played at most a limited role in economic development while in the Third World its role is central. The difficulty is that neither of these two, and few among innumerable similar claims, are true in general of either group of countries.[19]

The first claim is that the state in Western Europe was the creation of the ascendant bourgeoisie. O'Donnell [1980: p. 718], for example, sees the distinctness of the "periphery" as follows: "Contrary to the classic capitalist pattern of economic development, an emerging dominant class did not shape the political power embodied in the state." Alavi [1972: p. 61] thinks that "The essential problem about the state in post-colonial societies stems from the fact that it is not established by an ascendant native bourgeoisie but instead by a foreign imperialist bourgeoisie." One could obviously quarrel over the meaning of words such as "shape" or "establish" but the fact is that in Europe the bourgeoisie neither built the state nor ruled. Most of the building was done by bureaucracies and most of the ruling by absolute rulers, aristocracies, or armies. Had the Western European experience been one of strong bourgeoisies and instrumental states, the juxtaposition would have been obvious. But even if the English, French, and Prussian bourgeoisie were strong, they did not rule directly except perhaps for twenty years in France. The state was autonomous in most "classical" cases as it is in some less developed countries and the emphasis on the weak bourgeoisie has no explanatory punch. The state under capitalism seems to be most often autonomous, whether the bourgeoisie is strong or weak.

The second claim is that the role of the state is more central and active in the Third World than in the "classical" case. According to

Alavi [1972: p. 62], "The apparatus of the state, furthermore, assumes also a new and relatively autonomous *economic* role, which is not paralleled in the classical bourgeois state. The state in the post-colonial society directly appropriates a very large part of the economic surplus and deploys it in bureaucratically directed economic activity in the name of promoting economic development" [Also Saul, 1979]

Note that the "classical" case is now reduced to England. Even so, this claim is more difficult to evaluate, in part because historians have been changing their mind about both the English and other experiences and in part because the economic role of the state is neither uniform nor stable. The current view of the development of capitalism in England emphasizes the role of the state in destroying old property rights and securing new ones, in creating the market, and in regulating the labor force. According to the authority on England in Cippola's *Economic History of Europe*, "Historically, the most important way in which the state stimulated industrial growth in a capitalist setting was through its ability to restructure the institutions of society — i.e. through its ability to *create* a capitalist setting in the first place." [Supple, 1973: p. 307]. The central role of the state among the European late industrializers as well as in Japan needs no reminding. And, on the other side, at least in the light of orthodox historiography, the state in Argentina, Mexico, or Peru played almost no economic role during the latter part of the nineteenth century. It assumed an active role only after the crisis of 1929 and it became a major producer only in some countries and only recently. Outside the socialist bloc, the countries where the public sector produces the largest share of the gross national product today include Brazil, India, Austria, and Italy: a list which does not say much for juxtapositions between center and periphery.

In general, no contrasts can be sustained at this level: neither the role of the bourgeoisie in state building nor the role of the state in economic development have been the same all over Europe and they have not been uniform elsewhere, not only in the "Third World," whatever that is, but not even within Latin America, Africa, or Asia. Indeed, with regard to the Third World, O'Donnell [1980: p. 721] developed a set of rather fine categories for differentiating patterns of state formation. Structural differences among countries — differences created by the mode and the timing of insertion of particular countries into the international economic system — were crucial to the analysis of dependency of Cardoso and Faletto [1979 (1969)]. Bennett and Sharpe [1980] have shown that the Mexican state played a decisive economic role when the private sector was weak and that it has reduced the scope of its activities when the private sector developed. Evans [1985] has recently posed a number of subtle questions concerning the effects of internationalization of capital on the autonomy of the state in the center and in the periphery.

The fragility of generalizations concerning "the classical case" puts in doubt the explanation of state autonomy by the weakness of the bourgeoisie: if in England, France, and Prussia strong bourgeoisie did not take it upon themselves to rule, then the weakness of the bourgeoisie is not a necessary condition for state autonomy.[20] But neither is it a sufficient condition, since all that the weakness of the bourgeoisie can explain is that there is a power space to be filled but not that it is filled and how. Unless the strong bourgeoisie itself creates an autonomous state — a possibility which even the abdication theory does not entertain — some "state centric" elements must be called upon to explain why the state becomes autonomous and why it is organized in a particular way. We return to this theme below (3.5) but first one more factor, thus far ignored, must be introduced.

3.3. State autonomy and class balance

The strength of the bourgeoisie is relative to classes and groups whose interests conflict with those of capitalists. The struggle for power was excessively costly for the mid-nineteenth century French bourgeoisie because the nascent working class and other groups were also present politically, both on the street and at the polls. The ability of the bourgeoisie to conquer and wield the state power depends on the strength of its opponents. Thus whether the bourgeoisie is strong or weak in terms of its economic position and its political skills and resources, if its opponents are also strong politically, the space is open for the state to become autonomous. State autonomy results from class balance: this is the orthodox marxist explanation of state autonomy.[21]

Class balance is a necessary condition of state autonomy: when the bourgeoisie is strong, the strength of its opponents explains why the costs of struggling for power are so high; when the bourgeoisie is weak, the weakness of its opponents explains why they are not able to conquer power.[22] Several notions of balance have been entertained: (1)

Marx in 1871 [1971] referred to the Second Empire as "the only form of government possible at a time when the bourgeoisie had already lost, and the working class had not yet acquired, the faculty of ruling the nation." Here the balance is "marco-historical": capitalism is already developed sufficiently for the proletariat to threaten the bourgeois rule but not yet sufficiently to conquer power. Given Marx's linear concept of history, this kind of a balance occurs only once in the development of a nation and in this sense it constitutes an exceptional situation. But there is nothing that would prevent it from lasting for a very long time. (2) Gramsci [1971] labeled the "catastrophic balance" a situation in which both classes would destroy each other if either attempted to establish its rule. Here state autonomy is thus a game-theoretic equilibrium: neither class wants to struggle for power given the anticipated retaliation by its opponent and the outcome is that the state dominates both classes. Gramsci did not specify what brings about such a situation but presumably it could be a recurrent one and he notes himself that it could last long. (3) Engels in an 1852 text attributed the balance of classes to exhaustion caused by the past conflicts. Presumably, such a situation could recur. (4) Finally, Engels in the same text as well as Marx in 1871 and in other texts spoke of class balance as an effect of state actions. In this case class balance is not the original cause of autonomy, even if states may perpetuate their independence when they divide and conquer.

Class balance may thus have different origins; it may constitute a unique period in the history of a nation or a recurrent situation; it may result from objective conditions or from strategic calculations. But whatever its origin, explanations of state autonomy in terms of class balance have a prima facie plausibility. The full theory is hence the following: If at any time one class is (1) economically dominant and if (2) it can be organized politically and if (3) the power of this class is not seriously contested, then this class wields state power.[23] If any of these three conditions is violated, a space is opened for state autonomy.[24]

The problem with this theory is not that it is false but that it is trivial, since the three requisite conditions are rarely, if ever, satisfied in history. Nevertheless, the orthodox marxist theory does not stop here. Additional hypotheses are derived by distinguishing the balance between a strong bourgeoisie and a strong proletariat from one between a weak, divided bourgeoisie confronted by weak "popular sectors." The strong-strong balance leads to fascism; the weak-weak balance to milder forms of state autonomy, such as "Bonapartism," "Ceasarism," "imperialism," or "populism." A typical statement of this theory, with all of its dogmatic overtones, was provided by Rein [1960: p. 1]: "Just as Bonapartism belongs to the first phase of the bourgeois-liberal revolution, so fascism is connected with the second phase, the proletarian-social revolution." An extensive discussion took place in Germany over the interpretation of fascism in terms of class balance [Dülffer, 1976; Griepenburg and Jaden, 1966; Mason, 1966 and a discussion thereof, 1968; Rein, 1960; Rubel, 1960.][25]

In the light of this interpretation, the difference between fascism and populism is that in the former the state rises above already formed and organized classes while in the latter it dominates and organizes societies where the class structure is undeveloped. To achieve and maintain independence when classes are already formed, the state must destroy their organization, which explains why the state itself must be strong, or at least thoroughly repressive. When classes are weak, the state can become autonomous without much resistance and repression. This is then the second hypothesis concerning state autonomy generated by marxist assumptions. This hypothesis is no longer trivial and, if the terms can be reasonably defined, it is empirically testable.

Note that the distinction drawn by this theory is not between Western Europe and the less developed countries but among finely distinguished class relations characterizing historical situations. Here the mid-nineteenth century France falls on the same side as the mid-twentieth century Argentina. In both cases the bourgeoisie and its opponents were relatively weak; the bourgeoisie was divided (industrial vs. financial, urban vs. pampean); the working class was weakly distinguished from other working people (*les classes labourieuses, sectores populares*). In both cases the autonomous state rose as a direct relation between a personalistic leader and a mass of underprivileged individuals who were unable to represent themselves through any mediating organizations. In both cases the state sought to incorporate workers through state created organizations. And both of these cases are distinct from, say, post-1973 Chile, where the first task of the dictatorship was to destroy powerful class organizations.

Implicitly, the theory reconstructed thus far fills three cells of a fourfold table: (1) a strong bourgeoisie confronting weak opponents wields state power directly; (2) the balance between a strong bourgeoisie confronting a strong proletariat results in fascism; and (3) the situation in which all classes are weak results in milder forms of state autonomy. The case that is left is one in which the working class is strong and the bourgeoisie weak. The orthodox marxist theory says nothing about it; presumably in this case a revolution would be expected. One might, however, bring into this framework O'Donnell's [1973] theory of the rise of bureaucratic authoritarianism. In O'Donnell's view, the bureaucratic authoritarian regimes appeared in Argentina and Brazil when the indigenous bourgeoisie was unable to cope with the task of investing in the producer goods industry and when the popular sectors were highly mobilized in pursuit of economic demands. One might consider this situation as one in which the bourgeoisie is weak and its opponents strong and thus complete the general framework. [Principal discussions of O'Donnell's theory include Collier, ed., 1979; Remmer and Merkx, 1982.]

3.4. State and society

Class relations provide an explanation of state autonomy. If a strong bourgeoisie does not encounter serious opponents, the state is instrumental. Otherwise, the state is autonomous and the form this autonomy takes depends on the relative strength of classes. Nevertheless, as it stands, this explanation relies on a functionalist jump. For the most that class balance can explain is why no single social force can organize and wield state power by and for itself; the most it can specify is what kind of an autonomous state is possible given class relations. But what guarantees that when a strong bourgeoisie is confronted by a revolutionary proletariat, the fascist or functionally equivalent state will materialize to perform its function? And what precludes a state that looks very much like a fascist one from emerging even if all classes are weak? The very hypothesis that class relations create a space for state autonomy implies that this space is not filled in a way determined by these relations. The relative autonomy approach cannot specify which particular state institutions will emerge and continue to develop. We thus need to return to the state.

As O'Donnell [1977a] observed, the bourgeoisie is the only economically dominant class in history which does not control the means of violence. The bourgeoisie cannot call upon organized force to stand up in defense of its interests whenever need be; it can only hope that the state would follow policies that protect capitalism. Military governments often do defend the status quo, repressing movements by peasants or workers, but at times they also launch "modernizing" revolutions that attack interests of landowners and capitalists, *vide* Nasser's Egypt or Velasco's Peru. Thus, while the likelihood and the form of military intervention in politics depends on the dynamic of class relations it is also shaped by the transformations of military institutions. To understand the relation between state and society one must take into account the dynamic of both. [O'Donnell, 1976; Wiatr, 1987].

Yet a return to the state is not an easy one. Note that the independent development of the state was not ignored by Marx [1934: pp. 104–105]: "This executive power with its enormous bureaucratic and military organization, with its vast and ingenious state machinery, with a host of officials numbering half a million, besides an army of another half million, this appalling parasitic body, which enmeshes the body of French society and chokes all its pores, sprang up in the days of the absolute monarchy. . . ." This apparatus continued to grow "in the same measure as the division of labour within bourgeois society created new groups of interest, and, therefore, new material for state administration. Every *common* interest was straightway severed from society, counterposed to it as a higher, *general* interest, snatched from the activity of society members themselves and made an object of government activity, from a bridge, a schoolhouse and the communal property of a village community to the railways, the national wealth and the national university of France." And, Marx concluded, "Only under the second Bonaparte does the state seems to have made itself completely independent."

I cite this text at length for it epitomizes the difficulty. If we want to understand why the state had become autonomous in mid-nineteenth century France, is this account not sufficient in itself? Note the revealing language: "the state seems to have made itself independent." The bureaucracy was established under Luis XIV, it continued to expand by developing new and absorbing old activities, and eventually it grew sufficiently to have made itself independent. Why bring in the entire complex apparatus of class analysis if the independence of the state can be explained by transformations of the state apparatus alone?

The difficulty becomes even more apparent in the literature on the colonial and post-colonial state. [Alavi, 1972; Chandra, 1980; Saul, 1974]. Here the argument runs as follows: In the metropolitan countries, the state was created by the native bourgeoisie and served its interests. This state — a developed administrative and coercive machinery — was transplanted by colonizers to societies where the bourgeoisie was "weak." Thus follows Alavi's central hypothesis: "If a colony has a weak and underdeveloped indigenous bourgeoisie, it will be unable at the moment of independence to subordinate the relatively highly developed colonial state apparatus through which the Metropolitan power had exercised dominion over it." [1972: p. 13][26]

Is the post-colonial state independent because the bourgeoisie is weak or because the state apparatus is strong? Note that the eclectic answer does little good: to say "because of both" may be saying one thing too many. It is instructive to compare the theory of the "overdeveloped state" with the dependency theory — a product of a continent where the colonial experience receded deeper into the past. Both theories agree that the state tends to be autonomous in the less developed countries. But the dependency theory explains state autonomy without reverting to any autonomous development of state institutions. It derives the possibility of state autonomy from economic disarticulation: Economic activities on the territory of a particular country are not integrated via the local markets; landowners are economically independent of each other [Furtado, 1963]; the local bourgeoisie is divided along sectoral lines and by its links with foreign capital. If the local bourgeoisie is indeed weak (and O'Donnell [1980: p. 721] argues that not everywhere in Latin America it was) and if other groups have no organized political presence, the state can be only autonomous. Thus the possibility of state autonomy can be deduced from class structure. But if one takes the "overdeveloped" state as the point of departure, then there is no need for any class analysis. Indeed, the notion of a "weak" bourgeoisie is simply redundant when the existence of an independent administrative and coercive apparatus is a given and particularly when the bourgeoisie itself, along with other classes, is seen as a creature of the state.

Thus, the relative autonomy approach can at most explain why and what kind of autonomous state is possible, while bringing in the state seems to obliterate any need for class analysis. The state-centric approach is seductive because it seems sufficient by itself. Yet this explanatory promise of the state-centric approach hinges on an assumption that appears dubious. We thus need to examine the "state-centric" approach more systematically.

3.5. The "state-centric" approach

Views of the relation between states and societies tend to be paradigmatic. The language in which causal questions are formulated, their meaning and their relevance, depend on basic theoretical postulates that organize a particular understanding. In contrast to the "relative autonomy" approach, the "state centric" perspective assumes the primacy of force in the shaping of society. The state organizes and exercises the monopoly of physical force over a territory and it is the, overt or covert, reliance on violence that guarantees its efficacy. Society — a particular form of culture, social organization, and economic interaction — is an effect. The role of force was considered central by Weber [1968 (1922), vol. 3, chapters 10–13] and Hintze [1975 (1897–1932)]. The causal role of the state was recently placed at the center of society by Birnbaum and Badie [1983], Krasner [1978, 1984], Katzenstein [1978], and Skocpol [1985]. The "state-centric" theory with the most explicit deductive structure is Lane's [1942, 1958, collected in 1979; also Tilly, 1985].

Lane begins by distinguishing "two kinds of enterprises: (1) those that produce protection and are called governments and (2) those that produce goods and other services and pay governments for protection." [1979: p. 2] Since violence is a source of increasing returns to scale, "the production of protection is a natural monopoly." [p. 23] By monopolizing violence over a territory, governments establish property rights and make possible the development of society. The manner in which the state extracts resources from society largely determines what uses are made of scarce resources. Indeed, Lane concludes, governments "affected the extent to which monopoly prevailed in other fields of production, and in this way affected human relations throughout the whole economic organization." [1958: p. 416]

State-centric theories assert that states create, organize, and regulate societies. States dominate other organizations within a particular territory, they mold the culture and shape the economy. Thus the problem of the autonomy of the state with regard to society has no sense within this perspective. It should not even appear. The concept of "autonomy" is a useful instrument of analysis only if the domination by the state over society is a contingent situation, that is, if the state derives its efficacy from private property, societal values, or some other sources located outside it. Within a true "state-centric" approach, this concept has nothing to contribute. Indeed, writers who take as the central feature of the state its monopoly over the means of violence eschew the concept of "autonomy" altogether.[27] "Domination" is the term which for them describes the relation of the state to society, not "autonomy."

What is problematic in this perspective is the emancipation of society from the state. "Liberties," Lane notes, appeared originally as privileges of non-interference by the state. Morality and religion became private matters as the society emancipated itself from the state; "civil society" emerged as an autonomous sphere from under the control of absolutist rule [Poggi, 1978, chapter 4]. The origins of democracy are explained here by calculations of self-interested rulers: the relevant question is whether revenue maximizing rulers prefer to rely on taxation with consent rather than on extraction by the threat of force. Lane's answer is that democracy appears, "when technological improvements — industrial innovations — become more important than protection rent as a source of business profits" [1958: p. 412]. North [1984] and Bates and Lien [1985] give similar answers which focus, respectively, on transaction costs and on deadweight losses from extraction. Thus, in the course of historical development society gains independence from the state: this is the direction of causality within the state-centric approach.[28]

From what does the state derive its power in the state-centric approach? In the German "military" version, as well as for Lane, the answer is explicit and simple: from being able to use and to threaten the use of violence. It is the monopoly of violence that equips the state with its specific efficacy against all other social organizations. As Mann [1984: p. 186] notes, in this perspective "The state is still nothing in itself: it is merely the embodiment of physical force in society." The state is the center of society because physical force is the center of the state.

This reductionism is not of itself objectionable, particularly in the milder versions of this approach, where some form of consent or legitimacy cloaks the physical force under normal circumstances. But the thesis that the state derives its power exclusively or ultimately from the monopoly of force is unconvincing, for two reasons.

The empirical puzzle for this approach lies in the structure of the state itself, specifically, in the incidence of civilian control over the military: there are quite a few societies where persons and institutions other than hierarchical military commanders are able to rule. One could treat these instances as epiphenomenal, arguing that physical force will invariably come to the fore whenever other mechanisms of domination fail: Gramsci [1971], for example, maintained that hegemony is always protected by the armor of coercion. Even then, the question would remain why those who hold the monopoly of violence want to revert to these kind of appearances. But given that in several societies, over extended periods of time, the organized forces of coercion played a minor role within the state, the assumption that the power of the state always and everywhere ultimately stems from physical force strains credulity.

The second reason why this thesis is unpersuasive lies in the structure of the capitalist economy, in which decisions about allocating resources are made in a decentralized manner and in which owners of endowments, capital and labor, can withdraw them from productive uses. A state based on force may be perhaps able to centralize the economy, to expropriate labor and capital, but it cannot mandate allocations of resources as long as allocation decisions remain a private prerogative. In a decentralized economy force cannot be sufficient to rule effectively.

The monopoly of physical force is not the only conceivable source of state power. States may derive power from the need of societies for the performance of some tasks, whatever they are, that can be performed only on universalistic bases. Following Mann [1984], this could be called the "infrastructural power" in the sense that it constitutes the cost to society members of, broadly speaking, infrastructural services of the state, including protection. States may also derive power from values which lead individuals to recognize their authority, legitimacy, etc., that is, values which lead individuals to comply with their decisions in the absence of utility and physical coercion [Weber]. This is the "normative power." Finally, and perhaps paradoxically, they may derive power from constituting the arena of conflicts among other organizations [Poulantzas, 1978; Mann, 1984]. I will call this the "universalizing" power, for it rests on the capacity of states" (1) to invoke a superior interest, which transcends those of the other parties involved, and (2) to extract the sources that will make possible its attempts to resolve the issues raised" [Oszlak, 1981: p. 13].[29]

Note that all these powers are probably characterized by increasing returns to scale: hence, like violence, they constitute natural monopolies. But only physical force can assure that the state would be internally cohesive and externally effective in the face of conflicting interests. Unless the power of the state rests on physical force, its internal cohesion and its external effectiveness are contingent in part on societal conditions, whether the economy, the value system, or collective conflicts. If state power is not based on force, state managers must observe and obey multiple constraints which originate within and outside state institutions.

Thus the state-centric approach is not coherent unless the power of the state is derived from physical force. By a state-centric or "statist" [Krasner, 1984] approach, I mean more than calls for taking state institutions into account in political analyses and more than denials of the sort "Political outcomes cannot be adequately understood as simply reflection" of this or that. When based on the assumption of the primacy of force, the statist approach constitutes a true paradigm: it has the effect of making other factors irrelevant, of making the relative autonomy approach redundant if not useless. When the power of the state rests on force, the state itself is a cohesive institution, capable of performing as an actor not only against external enemies but vis-a-vis the society. But if the cohesion and the effectiveness of the state are even in part contingent on conditions located within the society, then the state-centric approach cannot be sustained as a distinct paradigm.

3.6. State autonomy as a contingent outcome of conflicts

The allocation and the price of state services among particular groups, the values which make their members comply or contest state regulation, as well as the very state institutions are objects of perpetual conflicts. These conflicts occur along three dimensions:

(1) One line of conflicts runs among state agencies themselves. As complex organizations, states always face problems of cohesion that result from the inevitably fragmentalized and sequential nature of decision making. According to Padgett [1981: p. 82], such organizations can be subject only to control that is "ecological," that is, "indirect control over the underlying premises of choice . . . rather than direct control over the process of selection itself." The cohesion of the state is further undermined by two external circumstances: the need to cope in a specialized manner with specific transformations of society and by relations of specialized agencies with interested outsiders.

(2) Another set of conflicts concerns the objectives which are to guide state actions. The perennial issue is which particularistic interests are to be given universalistic status by being assumed by the state: interests of the state as a whole, of its agencies, of some specific outsiders, or of coalitions between some state agencies and some organizations.

(3) This struggle has winners and losers and it is in the interests of groups which end up having little influence over the state to counteract to the extent possible the state actions. Thus, the third line conflicts confront state agencies against social agents whose interests are adversely affected by public policy. When the state is sympathetic to interests of some social groups, its policies encounter resistance among other groups. In the extreme, when the state is cohesive and state managers are self interested, the state may be confronted against the entire society.

These conflicts pit state agencies, staffs, bureaus and committees, against one another and against various categories and organized groups of outsiders, ranging across households, firms, voluntary associations, compulsory organizations, and mass movements. The objectives and the strategies chosen by each of these actors depend on the actions of others and on the changing conditions. State managers respond to the changing social environment. As Silberman [1982: p. 232] put it with regard to Japan: "if we view the bureaucracy as a complex organization seeking to establish and maintain itself over time as the authoritative institution . . ., then the seemingly arbitrary changes in the structure of authority may be seen as a consequence of the bureaucracy's attempt to resolve, as all organizations seek to do, the uncertainties of its environment."

As a result, the structure of the state changes in response to economic, cultural, or political transformations [Oszlak, 1981: pp. 12-13]. For example, as different regimes tried to control the working class in post-war Argentina, governmental agencies dealing with labor were shifted under Peron from the Welfare Ministry to a separate Ministry of Labor; they were moved into the Ministry of the Economy under the military government of Ongania [See Buchanan, 1983] In O'Donnell's [1977] felicitous phrase, "the map — the distribution and density — of the state institutions in each historical case is the map of the sutures" of past social conflicts. These are sutures, not scars: they are produced by responses to wounds; not by the wounds. The state need not and does not "reflect," "express," "manifest," or otherwise mimic any "underlying" conditions and yet it may change in response to external transformations if in pursuit of their own goals state managers behave as intentional actors under changing constraints. Thus, effects of economic, cultural, or other social transformations on the cohesion of the state, its functions, and its effectiveness depend on the objectives of state managers, the means at their disposal and the structure of state agencies. There is no reductionism here.

The conflicts over the cohesion of state institutions, over their functions and over their efficacy have no predetermined outcome. Their result may be "state-centric" under some historical conditions and "society-centric" under other circumstances: it makes little sense to label approaches by what should be outcomes of concrete investigations. In Japan, where the post-revolutionary state faced the constraint of a highly egalitarian value system, bureaucrats, who sought to acquire and maintain a monopoly over the process of decision making, solved the problem of authority by introducing a formalized structure of career advancement, coupled with universalistic recruitment and with a claim to the monopoly of expertise about public matters. In search of legitimacy, the bureaucracy was able to coopt the leadership of political parties, to extend its own principle of organization to private organizations, in particular large firms, and to exclude those social groups, labor and the small business sector which it could not bureaucratize. The result was a "bureaucratic state" that went far on the road to producing a bureaucratic society. [This account follows Silberman, 1982.] In contrast, as Schmitter [1986: p. 3] observed, in several Western European countries, the state lost its internal cohesion and its functional specificity. Indeed, even the "relative superiority of coercive power within a given territory and a legitimate authority to use that power . . . are subject to unprecedented contestation and restriction." There is no center of any kind here.

The conclusion is thus the following. The "state-centric" approach represents in fact a distinct paradigm when it is based on the assumption of the primacy of force over other state agencies and over the society. If physical force is the ultimate source of all power, then both the structure of the state and of society result from wilful acts of those who monopolize it, use it, and threaten with it. But if the power of the state rests not only on the monopoly of organized violence, then the structure of state institutions and their relations with society are formed in the interaction among a large variety of actors, under economic, cultural and political constraints. State autonomy is then one among possible outcomes of this interaction.

4. CONSEQUENCES OF STATE AUTONOMY

Paradoxically, while intense debates surround the origins of state autonomy, its effects seem to be taken for granted. Yet states can be autonomous in a variety of ways, with different consequences for public policies and societal welfare. Specifically, it can be shown that those autonomous states which have the property right to the fiscal residuum should be expected to act differently from those states which have the authority to make policy decisions but do not have that property right.

How does state autonomy affect policy outcomes? To provide analytical instruments, consider a general theory of pure types of states. The proposed theory is based on neo-classically inspired writings by economic historians, in particular Lane [essays collected in 1979; see also Ames and Rapp, 1977; Davis, 1980; Levi, 1981; North, 1981; and Tilly, 1985, who objects against the neo-classical framework] and some elements of Williamson's [1964; see also Furubotn and Pejovich, 1972] theory of the firm.

States differ in three characteristics: (1) property rights to the fiscal residuum, (2) locus of decisions concerning the variety and quantity of government activities, and (3) organization of production of services. Fiscal residuum is the difference between benefits and costs of state activities, whatever these are. This residuum may be considered legally to be the property of state managers, whoever they are, or of the citizenry in general. Authority to decide the kind and amount of services and goods to be provided by the state can reside either in the state apparatus, elected representatives, or citizens directly. Finally, services and goods may be either produced by the state apparatuses themselves, with state managers benefiting from the production, or contracted out to third parties and thus produced as a cost to the state.

Particular combinations of these characteristics define three types of state that are of interest. We will say that in a "Republic" citizens have the property right to the fiscal residuum, they or their perfect agents make decisions concerning the variety and quantity of government activities, and the production of services is a cost to the state. We will call the "Princedom" a state in which the managers have the right to the fiscal residuum, they decide variety and quantity of government activities, and they in turn bear costs of performing these activities. We will call the "Bureaucracy" a state in which the property right to the fiscal residuum resides with citizens, decisions about government activities are made by state managers who are not effectively supervised, and the services are produced by the state apparatus itself, the members of which benefit from this production. These characteristics of the three types of state are summarized in Table 1.

States provide services which increase the revenues of the private economy above the ("competitive") rate that would accrue to the available capital stock without them. The classical example is protection. The state provides armed ships which escort commercial vessels. The number of ships that would get through pirate infested waters without any protection defines the competitive rate of return. Protection increases the number of ships which complete the journey and to the extent that Venice protects her ships better than Genoa, Venetian merchants benefit from differential rent. Hence, the total return to capital is the sum of the competitive rate and the differential rate when applied to the capital stock. Note that the differential rent and thus the total benefit from government activities increases with their quantity.

States extract payments. They must do so because production of services is costly. We will call "taxes" all revenues received by the state. Any excess of extracted payments over costs constitutes "tribute," a rent extracted by the state. The extreme limit of tribute is when the state takes from the people all they have: this is "plunder."

States perform activities and extract payments. People benefit from these activities and they pay. With these assumptions we can now

TABLE 1
Types of State

Type of State	Property of fiscal residuum	Locus of decisions	Production of services
Republic	Citizens	Citizens	Costly
Princedom	State	State	Costly
Bureaucracy	Citizens	State	Beneficial

answer the following question: What is the level of state activity and the amount and form of payments by the people that are characteristic of each type of state? We will ask in particular whether the quantity of services is efficient and whether the payment is excessive.

Consider first a "Republic," in which citizens all vote simultaneously to choose from the conceivable alternatives the amount of government services and of payment. The citizens want to maximize their net benefit from government activities, that is, to choose the level of activities which maximizes the difference between benefits and costs. We have seen above [Part I, Section 2.1] that they will choose the level of state activity which is efficient from their point of view, that is, the level for which the marginal benefit equals the marginal cost. Having chosen the efficient amount of government services, citizens of the Republic will vote to pay the cost of production of services but not monopoly rent to the state. This then is the first conclusion: the government would be efficient and taxes limited to costs in a state in which the property right to the fiscal residuum rests with citizens, and in which decisions are made by citizens or their perfect agents and the production of services is costly to the state.

To underline the contrasts, consider briefly the other types of state. The Princedom is a state which has the legal right to the fiscal residuum. This state seeks to maximize its net revenue, that is, the difference between tax receipts and costs of activities. If the Princedom is unconstrained, either by the political power or by the economic decisions of taxpayers, this state chooses the efficient level of activities and then plunders. If the Princedom must for some reason stop short of plunder, the state supplies less than the efficient level of activities. Hence under this form of state autonomy, the size of the government is likely to be too small.

The Bureaucracy has no legal right to the fiscal residuum but has the authority to make decisions about government activities and it benefits from supplying these activities regardless whether they are useful to anyone else. Perhaps "*nomenklatura*" would be a better term, since this description fits well the Soviet model.[30] Bureaucracy chooses an inefficiently high level of activities and extracts through taxes the cost of these activities.

These conclusions are summarized in Table 2.

Here then are the principal hypotheses derived from this theory: (1) Whenever the property right to the fiscal residuum rests with the

TABLE 2
Policies of Different States

	Level of state activity	Level of extraction
Republic	Efficient	Cost only
Princedom	Efficient or less	Plunder or less
Bureaucracy	Excessive	Cost only

people, who decide directly or through perfect agents upon government activities, which are produced at a cost to the state, the level of government activity will be efficient and the payments extracted from the people will be limited to the real cost of these activities; (2) Whenever the property right to the fiscal residuum rests with the state, which decides upon activities and produces them at a cost, the level of activity will be efficient or smaller and the payment extracted will include a monopoly rent; (3) Whenever the property right to the fiscal residuum rests with the people but decisions about activities are made by state managers who benefit from government activities, the level of activities will be excessive and the payment extracted from the people will cover but be limited to the cost of this level. These hypotheses are deduced from assumptions summarized in Table 1.[31]

The main question that needs to be posed with regard to these pure forms of state is to what extent their policies would differ once state managers take into consideration constraints originating from the economy. Such constraints tend to be ignored in the writings that emphasize state autonomy. This is true of the economic history literature as well as of the analyses of budget maximizing bureaucrats. In Lane's [1979] model only the positive effect of protection on the economy is considered while in North's [1981] theory economic constraints are limited almost exclusively to those that affect the ease of collecting taxes. In turn, models of autonomous government under democracy tend to ignore the effects of inefficient supply of services by government upon the economy on the assumption that the particular bureaus or committees presumably internalize only a small part of such effects and thus need not be concerned about them.

If we assume that the state operates in an economy comprising agents, individual and collective, who have property rights to their own labor power and to alienable productive resources and who behave strategically in their self-interest, it will be apparent that any government is in numerous ways constrained by the responses, and even by the anticipations, of these agents to government policy. As Schumpeter argued in 1918 [1954: p. 21], any self-interested government must temper its temptation to prey on the economy. The question is whether the economic constraints are so compelling as to nullify the differences originating from the forms of state listed above or sufficiently slack to allow for institutionally caused differences in policy outcomes.

5. STATE AUTONOMY UNDER DEMOCRACY

5.1. Autonomous bureaus

The state is autonomous when state managers have goals of their own and the institutional capacity to make decisions and execute them. Some of the pure types of states discussed above are autonomous in this sense. According to several theories, however, the state is in various ways and to varying degrees autonomous — from voters, groups, or classes — even under democratic institutions [Krasner, 1978; Nordlinger, 1981; Poulantzas, 1973; Skocpol, 1985]. Even in a democracy, state officials — elected politicians and appointed bureaucrats — are not perfect agents of the public on whose behalf they perform responsibilities: they do not act in the best interest of citizens.

The issue of state autonomy arises in a democracy because government officials have the legal right to make certain decisions while they have no property right to the fiscal residuum that may result from government activities. The story of a bureau can be told simply: (1) Bureaucrats want various things for themselves and they care to some extent (from not at all to very much) about their contribution to public welfare. They are indifferent among various combinations of private rewards and public benefits. (2) Bureaucrats must obtain some rewards if they are to perform effectively for the public: hence, public benefit increases for some time along with the private reward of the bureaucrats. But as private rewards increase, they begin to eat into the benefits of the public. (3) Bureaucrats make decisions without perfect supervision so they can choose the alternative which maximizes their satisfaction. (4) This choice is not the optimal one for the public, which thus suffers from state autonomy.

In Figure 2 the benefit to the public ("fiscal residuum," B) is

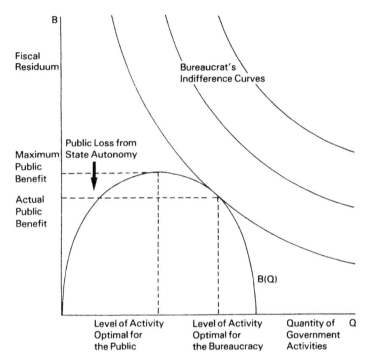

Figure 2

measured on the vertical axis. The horizontal axis measures the level of
government activity (Q, for "quantity"), since it is assumed that
private rewards of bureaucrats increase as government does more.
Bureaucrats are equally satisfied by all combinations of private
rewards and public benefits that lie along the same indifference curve
but they would like to have as much as possible of both. The function
B(Q) ("possibility frontier") describes the relation between the level of
government activity and public benefit. Public benefit increases at first
as rewards of bureaucrats (numbers of employed, salaries, facilities,
perks, etc.) increase. It reaches a maximum, and then declines as the
level of government activity continues to grow. At the maximum the
society benefits the most possible from government activities: this is the
social optimum or the efficient solution. If bureaucrats are not
perfectly monitored, however, they choose a level of activity which

maximizes their own satisfaction and this level exceeds the socially optimal one. Society suffers as the result.

What bureaucrats want for themselves is not exactly clear. According to Niskanen [1971], almost everything they want — salary, perks, power, patronage, and regulation although not the ease of managing and making changes — increases with the size of the budget; this is why Niskanen speaks about budget maximizing bureaucrats. According to Williamson [1964], managers in general like various perks which increase with the size of the staff and this assumption was applied to public bureaus by Migué and Bélanger [1974]. Parkinson [1957] thought bureaucrats like employing more labor; De Alessi [1969] saw them as biased in favor of more capital. The point is that whatever they want, they get it either by producing too much or too expensively or with a bias toward one factor.

Although the literature is enormous, this is not a complicated theory. Niskanen [1971] assumed that bureaucrats maximize budgets up to the constraint of allocations by committees and he discovered that bureaus overproduce services beyond the efficient point. Migué and Bélanger [1974] assumed that staff is not included as a cost when decisions are made and they discovered that bureaus will overstaff and thus produce both too much and too expensively. Orzechowski [1977] assumed that bureaucrats have a bias in favor of employing labor and he found you know what. Empirical studies comparing the efficiency, the cost, and the employment in public and private enterprises producing the same services tend to be poor methodologically since the direction of causality is difficult to determine: are private companies more efficient because they are private or are they private because they are more efficient? Sometimes one has the impression that desperation is involved in proving the point, for example, in a study which shows that, per unit of capital, public universities in the United States hire about 40 per cent more labor than private institutions — without controlling for the number of students [Orzechowski, 1977: p. 257].

5.2. Constraints

These models of autonomous bureaus pose almost no limits upon the behavior of bureaucrats. The question is how much autonomy would remain if some realistic constraints upon bureaucratic decisions were to be incorporated in the analysis. These constraints are threefold: (1)

supply side factors, that is, the costs of producing government services and of collecting revenues, (2) supervision by elected representatives or citizens directly, and (3) considerations originating from the economic system.

5.2.1. Supply Constraints   Supply constraints are numerous. They have received systematic attention particularly from North [1981]. Supply constraints become expressed as costs of producing services and of collecting taxes. These costs reflect difficulties in measuring output, monitoring transactions, extracting payments, etc. The classical example in history concerns the change in costs of warfare which resulted from the introduction of cannon and the consequent importance of infantry [Poggi, 1978; Schumpeter, 1954; Tilly, 1985]. *Ceteris paribus*, an increase in the cost of services or in the cost of collecting taxes will force bureaucrats to decrease their level of activity. Ward [1982] offered a theory of the growth of government formulated exclusively in supply terms: government expenditures grew because over time it became cheaper to collect taxes.

5.2.2. Institutional constraints   The constraints originating from supervision by elected representatives have received widespread attention. Two questions should be distinguished: whether bureaus can be effectively monitored by some other body, typically, the legislature and whether the supervisors themselves prefer an efficient outcome.

With regard to the relation between bureaucracy and legislature, the general conclusion of Miller and Moe [1983: p. 321] is persuasive: "Formal models of bureaucracy . . . have given undue emphasis to its independence, flexibility, and decisional control — and, in the process, either ignored or downplayed the capacity of legislature, specifically its committees, to act just as purposely and forcefully in achieving ends which may be quite at variance with those of the bureau." Let us follow Miller and Moe in their analysis and then generalize the problem out of the institutional context of the United States.

The critique by Miller and Moe is directed to Niskanen [1971] but it is valid with regard to the thesis of autonomous bureaus in general. For the glaring question is how do the bureaus escape supervision by elected representatives? In the Niskanen model, bureaus enjoy autonomy because (1) they have a monopoly on the supply of a particular service, (2) only they know the real costs of providing this service, and (3) they confront their legislative supervisors with an all-or-nothing choice. Niskanen's account of the budgeting process goes as follows: An oversight committee reveals how much it is willing to appropriate for each quantity of services; the bureau looks at its cost schedule, finds the maximum it can produce given what the committee is willing to pay, and communicates this amount to the committee, which then makes the final "decision." In fact, the only decision the committee makes is about its demand function. Once this decision becomes public, it is the bureau which decides how much will be produced, and we already know that it will produce as much as possible, beyond the socially efficient level. Miller and Moe point out that this account is based on peculiar assumptions and does not correspond to reality, specifically the reality of the United States Congress. Oddly, in the Niskanen model only bureaucrats are rational while legislators do not behave strategically. Moreover, in fact the committees, not the bureaus, make final decisions and the committees are not forced to choose between a level proposed by the bureau or nothing. Miller and Moe contrast the procedure described by Niskanen ("demand revealing oversight") with the other possibility ("demand concealing oversight"): the committee orders the bureau to inform it about the costs of producing particular amounts of services and the committee then picks the quantity that maximizes its own satisfaction [see also Breton and Wintrobe, 1975]. They retain Niskanen's assumption that the bureau can lie about the true costs and yet they obtain a truly powerful result: if the bureau is forced to provide a cost schedule without knowing the committee's demand schedule, the bureau will find it in its own best interest to reveal the true costs. Intuitively, the reason is the following. If the bureau lied to the committee by citing marginal cost above the true level, the bureau would choose the level of activity lower than under the true cost: something bureaus would want to avoid. If it cited marginal cost below the true level, the committee might choose the level of activity which the bureau could not in fact deliver. Hence, the Stackelberg strategy on the part of a bureau is to reveal true costs.

Thus, if the oversight committee is a perfect agent of the public, the outcome will be the socially optimal level of government activities. Translated into the general context of our discussion, this result is far reaching: even if the bureaucracy can hide real costs, it is sufficient that it be forced to reveal any supply schedule to the public or its perfect agents and the level of government activities will be efficient. Note that both Schumpeter [1954] and Poggi [1978: chapter 3] believe that the *Ständestaat* — a form of state in which, among other features, the prince had to turn to the estates with requests for specifically targeted funds — was efficient. The autonomy of bureaus is thus not inevitable.

The question that remains is whether committees are perfect agents of the public. Bureaucrats may be effectively supervised but the legislators who monitor their behavior may be also interested in programs that add up to an inefficiently excessive level of government activities. A series of analyses of the United States Congress demonstrated that under the particular institutional arrangement characterizing the United States electoral system and Congressional budgetary rules, legislators seeking re-election had good reasons to participate in vote trades that resulted in government overspending [Ferejohn, 1974; Fiorina, 1977; Shepsle and Weingast, 1981; Weingast, 1979]. Indeed, much of the American discussion is whether the bureaucrats or the legislators should be blamed for the alleged oversupply of services by the government [Weingast and Moran, 1983 is a recent illustration]. Miller and Moe distinguish whether legislative oversight is demand revealing or demand concealing, whether the service is provided by a government bureau or a private firm, whether the supplier is a monopolist or there is competition among suppliers, whether the oversight committee has a high demand for the particular service, and whether the legislature as a whole has a high demand for government services. Their conclusions show that while the Niskanen result is possible under some extreme conditions, under other conditions the bureaucracy may be forced to undersupply socially beneficial services and under still other arrangements it will supply services exactly at the socially optimal level. Thus whether bureaucrats are effectively supervised and whether supervision by elected representatives makes the final outcome efficient depends upon institutional factors specific to electoral systems, organization of legislatures, and powers of legislative committees with regard to bureaus.

5.2.3. Economic constraints Even autonomous states are constrained by the structure of property. The issue of economic constraints is discussed in the next section.

5.3. Unresolved issues

To analyze the possibility and the effects of state autonomy under democracy, we thus need the following model. There are voters, parties, elected politicians, and bureaucrats, each category with specific goals of their own, all embedded within particular institutions. They behave strategically with regard to one another. Institutions play a crucial role since they delimit and enable the feasible courses of action: for example, whether representatives will want to promote their districts or their party, whether representatives will be able to decide each spending item separately, whether a legislative committee will have the power to force the bureaucracy to reveal the supply schedule, whether and who will be able to control the agenda, etc. [See Fiorina and Noll, 1978.] Eventually, the particular institutional arrangements determine which kind of outcome is more likely, where these outcomes can be distinguished in general game-theoretic terms. Under some arrangements, bureaus and comittees may be able to reach a cooperative solution; under some arrangements the non-cooperative outcome in which everyone chooses their courses of action simultaneously (Nash) may be more likely. [In Miller's, 1977, general formulation this solution is socially suboptimal]. Under other institutions one party, legislators or perhaps even voters, will be able to force bureaucrats to reveal first their eventual reactions (Stackelberg solutions). Each of these solutions implies a different level of government activity and a different distribution of its costs and benefits.

Unfortunately, cross-national empirical evidence for this approach is almost non-existent. The topic of state autonomy suffers from a particularly large gap betwen theory and data. As shown above, the public choice approach generated a large body of theory, which is highly sensitive to institutional context and which implies predictions concerning patterns of government activities. Yet systematic empirical examination of these theories is limited to the United States, while cross-national research continues to be atheoretical. Following Nettl's [1968] seminal article, there is now an enormous body of writings concerning "weak" and "strong" states and "degrees of autonomy." [For recent reviews of this literature see Birnbaum, 1985; Skocpol, 1985.] Yet this literature is completely oblivious of public choice theory. It relies instead on inductive generalizations from the so-called "case studies" to illustrate the importance of state institutions for

policy formation. But many stories do not make a theory and we fail to
learn from these studies which specific aspects of state institutions
account for its autonomy. Thus all that can be said now is that state
autonomy is not inevitable under democratic conditions but particular
institutional arrangements may foster the autonomy of bureaucrats or
legislators or both.

This situation is particularly regrettable because the empirical
validity of the models arising out of public choice assumptions is far
from evident. Even the very core of the theory — the proposition that
government spending would be higher where benefits are concentrated
and costs are diffuse — fares badly in a simple confrontation with
cross-national data. For example, the public choice theory implies
[Fiorina and Noll, 1978: pp. 252–253] that ceteris paribus governments
should have grown larger in the plurality/majority than in the proportional representation systems. A quick calculation shows that between
roughly 1960 and 1979 total government expenditures increased on the
average by 8.5 per cent in five plurality/majority systems and by 18.3
per cent in ten proportional representation systems; by 1977–79 the
average level of total government expenditures was 38.8 per cent of
GDP in the first group of countries and 49.1 in the second. [Expendi-
ture data are from Schott, 1984: Table 3.6; information about electoral
systems is derived from Rae, 1971: Table 2.1.] Moreover, government
expenditure turns out to be higher by seven per cent in countries that
have a unitary rather than a federal system [Saunders and Klau, 1985:
p. 117]. When one reads the American literature on government
"overspending" one tends to forget that during the sixties and
seventies total government expenditures grew less in the United States
than in any other industrialized country and that among the OECD
countries only Japan and Australia now have lower government
expenditures.

6. CONCLUSION

The fundamental impression that emerges from the theoretical
analyses of relations among state institutions is not that the state is
necessarily autonomous but that these institutions lack a single
universalistic rationality that would both distinguish and separate them
from private and thus particularistic actors. The Hegelian and, in a

different way, the Weberian legacies left a vision of the state as a cohesive actor, imbued with a sui generis, universalistic, rationality, and charged with distinct functions. In various marxist analyses, particularly those of Poulantzas [1973] and the German capital logic school [Holloway and Piccioto, 1978], the state was treated as the unified actor which assured the cohesion of the social system as a whole. The Weberian tradition has been recently rediscovered by some sociologists who decided that the state is the "center" of society. This view of the state was challenged by various versions of capture theory which observed that the state was not cohesive because it was permeated by private actors with their particularistic interests. The implications of the public choice approach go even deeper. The cohesion of the state is always problematic for purely institutional reasons: the state is a complex system without a fixed center of cohesion. The problem with viewing the state as a center of anything else is that the state has no center itself. Indeed, as Schmitter [1986: p. 3] put it, the contemporary capitalist state constitutes "an amorphous complex of agencies with very ill-defined boundaries, performing a great variety of not very distinctive functions."

Part III: The Rule of Capital

1. INTRODUCTION

The central and the only distinctive claim of marxist political theory is that under capitalism all governments must respect and protect the essential claims of those who own the productive wealth of society. Capitalists are endowed with public power, power which no formal institutions can overcome [Luxemburg, 1970; Pashukanis, 1951]. People may have political rights, they may vote, and governments may pursue popular mandates. State managers may have interests and conceptions of their own. But the effective capacity of all governments to attain whatever goals is circumscribed by the public power of capital. The nature of political forces which control the state institutions does not alter this situation, for it is structural: a characteristic of the system, not of the occupants of governmental positions or the winners of elections.

According to marxist theories of the state which flourished during the 1960s and 1970s, the survival of capitalism has been possible only because of the role played by the state. Given the growth of monopolies, the falling rate of profit, the expanding scale of investments, the recurrent crises of demand, the increasing difficulties of legitimation and the militancy of the working class, capitalism could not survive without state policies promoting accumulation and legitimation. Conversely, all that states do, public policy in every realm and of every form, can be understood and predicted by assuming that state institutions function to reproduce capitalism. The basic structure of these theories and two most important versions are the subject of Section 2.

To account for state intervention, these theories must explain why all governments in capitalist societies are bound to act in the interest of capital, capitalism or capitalists. In one explanation, state managers internalize the goals of capitalists and use the state as an instrument on their behalf. Another explanation emphasizes institutional limitations: under capitalism, the state cannot organize production, it cannot mandate investment, it cannot command consumption because these are prerogatives reserved to owners. But the most daring, because the least contingent, theory claims that it does not matter who the state managers are, what they want and whom they represent. Nor does it matter how the state is organized and what it is legally able or unable to do. Capitalists do not even have to organize and act collectively: it suffices that they blindly pursue narrow, private self-interest to cause all governments to respect the limits imposed by public consequences of their private decisions. This is the theory of "structural dependence of the state on capital," discussed in Section 3.

The functionalist account of the survival of capitalism turns out to be unsatisfactory in a number of ways. The central difficulty is that this approach does not leave any role for conflicts, for strategic interactions among social forces. Workers appear in this account only as victimized by repression, misled by ideological domination or betrayed by leaders, Yet in many countries workers have been organized in unions and parties and their organizations have been pursuing strategies consistent with the continued existence of capitalism. Hence, in order to understand the longevity of capitalism, it is necessary to analyze it as an outcome of strategic interactions among collectively organized social forces. Section 4 reviews such analyses.

2. THE STATE AND REPRODUCTION OF CAPITALISM

According to Marx's theory of capitalism, as put forth in *Capital*, this system of production and exchange reproduces itself spontaneously, as an automatic effect of its functioning. The state may have been necessary to create capitalism during the period of "primitive accumulation" but, once in place, capitalism reproduces the conditions of its own existence. In contrast, regardless of the tone they assume toward Marx, from ostensibly exegetic to openly critical, all recent marxist theories of the state begin by asserting that one or another among the conditions necessary for reproduction are absent in contemporary capitalist societies. Either Marx had erred or capitalism had changed. Since some conditions necessary for the spontaneous reproduction of capitalism have been absent at least for several decades and since capitalism is still around, the inevitable conclusion is that some institutions outside the system of production and exchange must be doing whatever is required to maintain the capitalist system. These institutions are identified as the state. Thus the explanation for the persistence of capitalism in the face of various threats is to be found in the activities of state institutions. Conversely, all public policies can be understood, and predicted, by referring to the prerequisites of continued capitalist production. The function of the state is to reproduce capitalism and this is the goal of public policy.

Why would the state have to do anything to reproduce capitalist relations? Why wouldn't capitalism survive without state intervention? At a general level, marxist analysts of capitalism converge to the view that the survival, maintenance, viability, or reproduction of this system requires continued accumulation and legitimacy. Capitalism may undergo periodic crises during which production, employment or consumption temporarily decline but it cannot stagnate permanently; as Marx emphasized, capitalism must develop incessantly just to survive. Continued accumulation is thus the first necessary condition, the central functional requirement, for the reproduction of capitalism. Legitimacy is the second necessary condition, either because mass support is required by the rules of democracy or at least because consent is necessary to defuse the omnipresent revolutionary threat.[32] Accumulation and legitimacy are thus the functional prerequisites for the survival of capitalism and, for various reasons, accumulation and legitimacy are not, or no longer, generated spontaneously by capitalist economies.

Six major threats to accumulation and legitimacy are emphasized by various writers: (1) Competition among firms is insufficient to assure that all the activities necessary for continued capitalist production would be undertaken spontaneously. (2) The rate of profit has fallen, for reasons anticipated by Marx or because of wage pressure. (3) The capitalist economy does not provide enough public goods, the scale of which has increased beyond the capacities of private provision. (4) Surplus population does not function sufficiently as a reserve army; wages exceed subsistence and threaten profitability. (5) The capitalist system is threatened by political organization of all those whom it exploits or oppresses. (6) The non-economic conditions necessary for continued capitalist production and exchange, such as education, family patterns, motivations, etc. are not generated spontaneously by the mere fact that the economic system is organized as a capitalist one.

If the capitalist system of production and exchange has survived all these threats, some non-economic institutions must have been generating the conditions necessary for accumulation and legitimation. For various reasons, the state is the only institution capable of furnishing the missing conditions of continued capitalist production. Thus contemporary capitalism is in one form or another a "state capitalism": the active role of the state is the key to its survival. A typical early statement of this perspective was by Murray [1971: p. 87], who maintained that "contrary to liberal models, capitalism cannot be analyzed as a system without taking account of the role of the state, and that, more particularly, in the process of capitalist production and reproduction the state has certain economic functions which it will always perform, although in different forms and to different extents."

What must the state do to maintain capitalism? At the most general level, the answer is given directly by the two central functional prerequisites of capitalist reproduction: it must furnish the conditions necessary for accumulation and legitimation. All public policy constitutes attempts to implement these two objectives.[33] The objective of state institutions in all capitalist societies is to promote accumulation and legitimation or, to the extent to which these objectives are mutually contradictory, to maximize accumulation under the constraint of social peace.

Under concrete historical conditions, these objectives are

implemented by a number of "functions" which states must perform. Within this framework, state policies constitute "functions": activities of a part (the state) that have a stabilizing effect on the (capitalist) system as a whole. Although the particular formulations differ slightly, the list of functions offered by different authors is surprisingly uniform. Murray's [1971] functions included guaranteeing property rights, economic liberalization, intervention for social consensus, and management of external relations. This is more or less the standard diet. Others have gone into more details, emphasizing the need for the state to train labour force, to socialize expenses on research and development, to facilitate communication, and so on. Habermas' [1975] enumeration contains a litany of about 70 specific functions treated as illustrations of a supposedly even longer and open-ended series.

This is then the common structure of several marxist theories of the state: When some conditions for accumulation and legitimacy are absent and reproduction of capitalism is threatened, the state performs the functions necessary to furnish these conditions. Survival of capitalism is due to activities of the state. In turn, all public policy constitutes an effort to create the conditions necessary for the survival of capitalism.

Within this common structure, however, particular theories differ with regard to some fundamental assumptions and conclusions. Marxist theoretical discussion concerning the state was exceptionally prolific for about twelve years following 1968 and a number of positions on central issues have been put forth.[34] Indeed, many writings of that period were polemical and several topics were subject to fervent debates. Among systematic theories those of Offe and Habermas, on the one hand, and of Poulantzas, on the other hand, provide the sharpest contrast. Following a summary of Marx's view of reproduction in Section 2.2, these theories are discussed separately in Sections 2.3 and 2.4. Other views are introduced when the theory is critically evaluated in Section 2.5.[35]

2.1. Marx's theory of reproduction of capitalism

The state played no role in Marx's analysis of the capitalist economy. Although Marx purportedly planned to continue *Capital* with a volume devoted to the state, there is nothing he could have written.

According to the theory contained in the three volumes actually published, once in place, capitalism reproduced itself and developed "of itself," autonomously and spontaneously, without state intervention. Since all contemporary marxist theories of state begin by rejecting this assertion, we need to examine first Marx's view of capitalism.

Capitalism, according to Marx, is a form of economic organization in which (1) the productive wealth, the instruments of production, are owned privately and allocated to uses by their owners, (2) the same is true for the capacity to work, what Marx called "labor power", (3) some owners of labor power do not own instruments of production which would enable them to satisfy their own needs. Hence, under capitalism there is a capital market where owners of productive wealth move their resources in pursuit of profit and there is a labor market where some owners of labor power are forced to sell their services in order to survive. Production occurs when laborers exchange their capacity to work for a wage and when capitalists or their delegates, qua organizers of the process of production, succeed in extracting actual labor out of labor power. The wage is not a title to the specific output in the making of which particular individuals participate but a quantity of an abstract medium exchangeable for goods and services.

Suppose that this system is already in existence in a particular society. There are some people who must sell their labor services if they are to survive. There are others who own the instruments of production and other necessary inputs. Workers appear at factory gates and offer to perform labor services. Competing for employment, they bid down wages until the level of subsistence. They are hired and, under supervision, they perform labor services. The end result of this activity is some output which constitutes the property of the capitalist. Workers receive wages and consume them. Capitalists sell the output and replenish the instruments of production.[36] Thus, at the end of this cycle workers are left, as they were before, with wages which they consume and with their capacity to work, while capitalists are left, as before, with the instruments of production. Since workers must sell their labor power to survive, they reappear at the gates, bid down wages, perform labor, consume wages, and return to the labor market. Capitalists, in turn, appropriate the product, realize its value, replenish the instruments of production, and hire workers. This process repeats itself "of itself," as a market exchange.[37] "Capitalist production," Marx observed, "of itself reproduces the separation between labour-power and the means of labour. It thereby reproduces and perpetuates the conditions for exploiting the labourer." (1967 vol. I: p. 577).

Thus social relations under which capitalist production occurs are produced anew each time something is produced under these relations. Economic organization is a joint product with whatever else is the output of this organization. In Marx's words, "Capitalist production, therefore, under its aspect of a continuous connected process, of a process of reproduction, produces not only commodities, not only surplus-value, but it also produces and reproduces the capitalist relation: on the one side the capitalist, on the other the wage labourer." (vol. I: 578)

Once particular commodities are produced, the second stage of reproduction begins. In Marx's account, "The conditions of direct exploitation, and those of realizing it [surplus value] are not identical. They diverge not only in place and time, but also logically." (vol. III: 244) Firms realize the value of commodities by exchanging with each other and selling to workers. Firms compete with each other and they move resources to maximize profit. As a result, the rate of profit tends to be uniform across sectors and, most importantly, all activities that are productive (in the sense that they yield a positive rate of return at subsistence wage; see Morishima, 1973) are undertaken. Hence, competition is sufficient for the economy to reproduce itself as a complex system of division of labor.[38]

Finally, according to Marx, institutional, legal and ideological conditions necessary for a continued functioning of any economic system also spontaneously repeat themselves, again "of itself." "It is furthermore clear that here as always it is in the interest of the ruling section of society to sanction the existing order as law and to legally establish its limits given through usage and tradition. Apart from all else, this, by the way, comes of itself as soon as the constant reproduction of the basis of the existing order and its fundamental relations assumes a regulated and orderly form in the course of time." (vol. III: 793)

In sum, Marx believed that, once established, capitalism reproduces itself automatically, as a spontaneous effect of decentralized decisions of workers and capitalists. Capitalist relations reproduce themselves at the micro-level since class relations are produced each time anew as a joint product with the commodities. Competition guarantees that the capitalist economy reproduces itself as a complex system of division of labor. Ideological and legal conditions necessary for capitalist production are themselves recreated as an effect of the economic relations which they institutionalize. And, again as an unintended by-product, the capitalist system reproduces among individuals the kind of ("fetishized") knowledge which is necessary for them to function effectively within this system.

Thus, while both Marx and Engels wrote at times that the capitalist economy requires specific "external conditions," in Marx's theory capitalism reproduced itself endogenously. The state was not needed for anything, not even to ward off the revolutionary threat by workers. Given the lip service marxists often pay to "class struggle," this observation may strike one as improbable. Yet class struggle plays no systematic role in Marx's theory of capitalism. Capitalism reproduces itself and develops by virtue of its organization. The role of class conflicts is at most to accelerate or retard the lawful developments. Class conflict in *Capital* is thus at most a source of deviations from laws, and theories are about laws, not about deviations. In Marx's theory, workers compete with each other as individuals. This competition is sufficient to maintain wages at the level of subsistence and to ward off any threat that might result from collective action.

One might think that this self-reproducing capacity is inherent in any system of economic organization. Yet in Marx's view, capitalism is the only system which has this feature. For contrast, consider feudalism. There a peasant starts with wheat growing on his field; he can harvest the wheat, feed himself and his family, and use the rest of the grain as seed; and he can go on repeating this cycle. If the peasant pays rent to the feudal lord, it is because of some factor of an extra-economic nature: threat of force, religious convictions, some other normative or habitual force.[39] The feudal economic system is reproduced only because this non-economic element enters into each cycle of production; without it, peasants would retain the entire crop, the lord would starve, and feudalism would be over.

Describing the transition from feudalism to capitalism, Marx noted at one point that the "medieval proverb '*nulle terre sans seigneur*' was replaced by that other proverb, '*l'argent n'a pas de maître*.'" Reproduction of capitalism does not require interventions of the state into the particular cycles of production.[40] Capitalism is a self-reproducing system.[41]

2.2. Offe and Habermas

Both Offe and Habermas seem to agree with Marx's analysis of competitive capitalism.[42] They begin from the assumption that if market relations were universal and competitive, capitalism would have worked smoothly, that is, (1) accumulation would proceed steadily, (2) there would be sufficient legitimacy and (3) the state would not lack material resources and mass support [Offe and Ronge, 1975]. According to Offe [1975: pp. 6–7], when "the commodity form does govern all social relationships permanently, there is neither a problem of accumulation (which is nothing but the by-product of equal exchange of equivalents between labor and capital) nor a problem of legitimation (which would be provided by the 'justice' of the market place, namely equivalent exchange)." All this was true of "liberal capitalism" [Habermas, 1975: pp. 20–33]. The state provided external conditions of production and, since "the law of value operated," everything else came of itself. Accumulation proceeded smoothly. The market performed its double cybernetic function: it allocated labor and reproduced classes. Finally, the market was self-legitimating.[43]

What happened to liberal capitalism is not easy to decipher. It vanished: Habermas says that we know why and how.[44] At first oligopolies and monopolies appeared: "The spread of oligopolistic market structures certainly means the end of *competitive capitalism*" [1975: p. 33]. But the market still steered investment, until it developed "functional gaps." Then the state stepped in and, by means of global planning, it replaced the market. From this moment the law of value no longer operates. The market loses its steering capacity. Resources are allocated to uses by administrative decisions. Wage structure becomes "quasi-political": wages are determined by conflicts among organizations, not by the value of labor power. Finally, along with its steering function, the market loses its legitimizing capacity. In the end, the "late," "organized," or "state-regulated" capitalism has nothing in common with the liberal, competitive era. Even if Marx had been correct about his era — and the references to "the law of value" would indicate that he was — his theory is no longer relevant for contemporary capitalism, which no longer organized by the market but by the state.[45]

Offe's diagnosis of what ails late capitalism is more pointed. According to Offe, capitalism exhibits a permanent tendency toward "decommodification": labor power and alienable resources tend to be withdrawn from exchange or exchanged through non-market mechanisms. Thus the scope of market relations becomes reduced as the normal consequence of market operation. Like Habermas, Offe is not quite certain why this decommodification originally occurred. Monopolies are one likely culprit, public goods another, but there are other candidates. The fact is that this tendency toward decommodification creates problems for capitalism: when capital and labor power escape from market exchange, accumulation is no longer automatic, legitimation is threatened, and the state is deprived of resources and support. Thus is born "the problem of the capitalist state" [Offe and Ronge, 1975].

In order to understand why and how governments respond to this inadequacy of the market, we need to note four features of the state in any capitalist society: (1) The state normally does not engage in production (and when it does, it behaves like private actors). (2) The state derives its resources from the economy where decisions follow private rationality. (3) The state is compelled to be concerned with accumulation as the source of its own resources. (4) Not having any sources of power of its own, governments must be concerned about securing legitimacy and under democracy they must seek electorally expressed support. Accumulation and legitimation are thus the central functional problems of any state in a capitalist society. Conversely — here we have first consequences of these assumptions — all public policy is to be understood as a response of the state to the requirements of accumulation and legitimation. Note that these requirements do need to be reconciled: legitimation is costly and the cost is expressed in accumulation. [This was the specific contribution of O'Connor, 1973.] As Habermas put it, "Because a class compromise has been made the foundation of reproduction, the state must fulfill its tasks in the economic system under the limiting conditions that mass loyalty be simultaneously secured within the framework of a formal democracy and in accord with a universalistic value system." [1975: p. 58] Hence the objective of the state under late capitalism: maximize accumulation under the constraint of maintaining legitimacy.

The thorny problem which all theories with similar structure encounter at this moment — the problem discussed separately below — is to explain why the particular individuals who under concrete circumstances occupy places within state institutions undertake actions oriented to fulfill the requirements of capitalist reproduction. Offe's answer relies on two mechanisms: (1) state managers are compelled to promote accumulation and secure legitimation in their "institutional self-interest" and (2) under capitalism the state is organized as an institution in ways that preclude it from undertaking some actions that would change the character of the economy. The first point is made repeatedly but the causal chain is far from clear, in Offe's rendition as well as elsewhere, e.g. Lindblom [1977] or Block [1977, 1980]. The second point was a subject of a separate article [1974]. Perhaps the clearest summary of both is this passage: "the political system can only make offers to external, autonomous bodies responsible for decisions: either these offers are not accepted, thus making the attempts at direction in vain, or the offers are so attractive in order to be accepted that the political direction for its part loses its autonomy because it has to internalize the aims of the system to be directed." Because the state cannot produce itself and because it needs production for all of its goals, it is dependent on satisfying interests of private decision makers.

What does the state do to promote accumulation and to secure legitimation? Habermas [1975: p. 51] provides an all-encompassing list of state functions. The state began by constituting and complementing the market. Eventually, it assumed the responsibility for managing the economy and for compensating those who are adversely affected by its operation. Each of these functions translates into a large number of tasks. As a result, the list of functions is long: almost everything governments ever do is a "function" of the state in late capitalism.

Offe's contribution is again more precise: states must pursue policies of "administrative recommodification," that is, measures oriented to strengthen the market and to extend the realm of market relations. "The basic hypothesis derived from these considerations" he writes, "is that state policies consist in series of measures which facilitate exchangeability of production factor. . . ." [1975b: p. 9] Formulated in the mid-1970s, this hypothesis may have not been very persuasive but it turned out to be prophetic: the central thrust of political change during the last decade has been to commit governments, in the United States and in Europe, to "administrative recommodification." [See OECD, 1983a.] Offe's general statement is exemplified by a number of specific "functions of the state" but these are less interesting.

This is then the Offe–Habermas theory of the state under late capitalism: Since the capitalist market is not a self-perpetuating institution, because of its vulnerability to monopolization and decommodification, the state must replace the market in allocating resources to productive uses and in distributing income. The function of the state is to promote accumulation while maintaining legitimacy and all public policy should be viewed as an effort to implement these objectives.

The distinctive contribution of Habermas and Offe lies in the consequences they derive from this theory in the search for limitations and contradictions of public policy. The basic thesis they share is that attempts to resolve current problems create new, often more profound ones. The general model runs as follows: (1) Because the market develops "functional gaps," the state must intervene. (2) By intervening, it politicizes economic relations: relations of power replace those of exchange. (3) Politicization of economic relations leads to new crises and may cause failures. In Habermas' view, capitalism can function only if it disposes of "requisite quantities" of consumable values, rational decisions, generalized motivations, and action-motivating meanings. While state management of the economy is made necessary by the inadequacy of the market in generating accumulation, the politicization of economic relations creates new problems of rationality, legitimacy, and motivation. A possibility of failure is thus permanently open: either because the state would be incompetent or unable to solve a current problem or because in coping with this problem it would create a new, insurmountable one.

The problems caused by the politicization of economic relations include irrationality of administrative decisions due to the capture of the state by private interests, the fragility of the "welfare state," and delegitimation. Fiscal crises, planning failures, and erosion of motivation of economic actors complete the list but their analyses differ less from other similar diagnoses.

When the state takes over the management of the economy, it becomes permeated by outside interests. Instead of an autonomous institution devoted to universalistic values, it becomes an arena for conflicts among all kinds of interests. Thus Habermas observes that "Contradictions among the interest of individual capitalists, between individual interests and the collective-capitalist interest, and finally, between interests specific to the system and generalizable interests, are displaced into the state apparatus." [1975: p. 60] Moreover, under democratic conditions the state apparatus is likely to act in pursuit of political support rather than be concerned with accumulation. In Offe's view, there "is the very real possibility that in order to retain their very capacity of control (derived from political power and legitimacy), the state agencies will feel compelled to block the very purpose of use-value production strictly complementary to capital accumulation by giving in to the claims which emerge merely from party competition and political conflict, but in no way directly result from the actual requirements of accumulation itself. The consequence would be not 'symbiotic' complementarity but 'parasitic' self-sufficiency and autonomy of state infrastructure production." [1973, I: p. 115] Thus the state which replaces the market to organize accumulation need not be any more successful in its task.[46]

The most original of Offe's contributions is perhaps his understanding of fragility of the "welfare state," which follows from the theory of "decommodification." [The first statement is 1972c.] He maintains that those services which eventually became organized by the "welfare state" were in fact a pre-condition for the labor market to emerge: only when certain (household, education, etc.) activities are performed outside the labor market, that is, outside the realm of exchange based on value, can individuals sell their labor services. The existence of social spheres not based on market exchange is thus a precondition for the existence of markets, in particular of the labor market. In the course of history, the provision of welfare became politicized and extended, first by the parliaments and elections, then by corporatist institutions. But while the growth of non-exchange systems is necessary for markets to exist and to function, this development takes away resources and decreases efficiency: on the latter point, Offe shares another conclusion of conservative analyses. The state is thus permanently caught between the need to re-commodify and the need to withdraw resources from market exchange and make decisions by non-market criteria. This contradictory function of the welfare state explains its political fragility [1984].

Offe's analyses of problems of legitimation parallel those of Habermas. The market is a self-legitimizing institution because individuals confront only themselves and an impersonal mechanism: they can understand their achievements and failures only in terms of their own performance or, at most, luck. But once the state began to manage the economy, economic relations became politicized. Economic outcomes began to depend on specific decisions of identifiable institutions, parties or even individuals. People can find culprits for their misery and take political actions against them. Markets no longer legitimize while political relations are transparent. Now every economic crisis becomes at the same time a political one (although there are obviously other sources of political crises). Thus, states which intervene in the economy create problems of legitimation. Eventually they encounter tensions between promoting accumulation and securing legitimation, since they must take resources away from accumulation to compensate those individuals who lose in the economic game. Fiscal crises constitute one expression of this contradictory task faced by the state.

Although both devote extensive attention to legitimation, one aspect of the entire problematic of legitimacy is left ambivalent both by Habermas and Offe,: the relation between legitimacy and democracy. Herbermas argues that legitimacy is not generated by legality alone: thus presumably liberal democracy is not sufficient to guarantee legitimacy. But why should states under capitalism be necessarily concerned with legitimacy at all? In fact, both Habermas and Offe seem to limit their analysis to democratic capitalism and both ignore the role of repression as an alternative to legitimacy. But even with regard to democratic conditions, they do not distinguish between governments seeking political support to win re-election, states seeking mass support for the political system, and states seeking legitimacy for capitalism. Habermas' opus on the state bears the title *Legitimation Crisis* but in the end it is far from clear what the referent of this crisis is supposed to be.

While state intervention is necessary to reproduce capitalism and this intervention creates in turn problems of its own, we do not know, and cannot know a priori, whether and when state intervention will end up in a failure. We know the state is likely to goof from time to time: "To assume that the state infrastructure will prove capable of effectively discerning and overcoming functional gaps in the accumulation process in terms of quantity, quality and timing," Offe writes, "would mean to overestimate both the diagnostic and prognostic capacities of infrastructure policy as well as the political and financial leeway it disposes of." [1973, I: p. 115] In the end, we do not even know whether state intervention does more good than harm to capitalism: "The question that remains unanswered, left solely to contingencies, is whether the intervention of any 'separate' sector of the state to counteract the functional gaps arising in market-controlled capital accumulation process will in the long run serve to stabilize or to jeopardize this process." [1973, I: p. 111] For a theory which seeks to explain reproduction of capitalism, this is a meek conclusion.[47] One would expect that such a theory would at least specify the conditions under which the state should be expected to fail in its task of maintaining capitalism, rather than leave this possibility to residual contingencies. This difficulty, however, is not particular to the Offe–Habermas version of theories of state.

2.3. Poulantzas

While Habermas and Offe almost never explicitly refer to Marx but in fact assume that Marx was correct in his analysis of reproduction under liberal capitalism, Poulantzas presents his views as interpretations of Marx but in fact rejects two central aspects of Marx's account of reproduction.[48] Specifically, while Habermas and Offe assume that competitive capitalism would have been, or was, self-reproducing, Poulantzas argues that capitalism can never reproduce itself without the state. One reason is that non-economic conditions necessary for capitalist production and exchange are not generated spontaneously by the operation of the economic system. In Poulantzas' language, "the unity of the formation is never given by the economic alone." [p. 45] The second reason is that capitalism always faces the potential threat from the working class. While for Offe and Habermas legitimacy becomes problematic only when the market fails to assure accumulation, for Poulantzas capitalism is never legitimate.[49]

As we have seen, Marx thought that legal and ideological institutions functional for each economic system arise spontaneously once a particular mode of production and exchange becomes routinized. This observation and an even stronger programmatic statement of the same principle in the *Critique of the Political Economy*, according to which even language and consciousness change rapidly with the change of the system of production, became enshrined by orthodox marxism as a "law of the necessary correspondence between the base and the superstructure." This "law" became the focus of Althusser's [1970, 1971] critique of stalinism. According to Althusser and his followers, Poulantzas among them, the way in which different social (that is, differentiated and interdependent) activities are organized need not be mutually re-enforcing, and this includes the system of production. Poulantzas [1964] applied this idea to the analysis of law. The law,

Poulantzas argued, constitutes a coherent system, which can change only according to laws without losing its coherence. Two consequences follow. First, contrary to stalinist theory, the bourgeoisie cannot use as instruments particular laws without breaking the entire system of law and thus rendering it ineffective. Secondly, the legal system changes not only in response to external conditions but also according to its own logic. Hence, law is a "relatively autonomous instance" and different instances "develop unevenly." Given the "relative autonomy of instances" and their "uneven development," there is no prior reason why "external conditions" of the capitalist economy should exist just because the economy is capitalist. Extended families, vocational schools or moral norms which condemn sex during daytime may be all necessary for capitalist production and exchange but a particular capitalist society may develop nuclear households, liberal education, and spontaneous sex.

Since capitalist production and exchange can continue only if other social activities are organized in some definite manner, it falls upon the state to assure the functionality of these activities with regard to the capitalist economy.[50] "Within the structure of various levels separated by unequal development," Poulantzas claimed, "the state has the particular function of being the factor of cohesion. . . ." [p. 43] If the various activities socially organized in a capitalist society cohere, it is only because of the state. The state is "a factor of 'order,' 'the principle of organization,' of a formation, not only in the ordinary sense of political order, but in the sense of cohesion of the levels of a complex unity and as the factor of regulation of its global equilibrium as a system." [p. 44] The state is "the organization for the conservation of the conditions of production and as such of the conditions of existence and functioning of the unity of a mode of production and of a formation." [p. 51]

What does the state do in order to regulate the cohesion of capitalist societies? It "intervenes." Besides a few platitudes, some of them referring ad hoc to the falling rate of profit, Poulantzas, who had a pronounced aversion to economics, did not even try to specify what the state may be called upon to do in the economic realm in order to preserve capitalism. His numerous followers specialized in case studies of public policies, which showed invariably that the state did whatever was necessary, the necessary being what it did.[51]

The interest of Poulantzas' theory lies in his analysis of political functions of the state, in particular with regard to the bourgeoisie, and in his attempt to explain why the working class does not overthrow capitalism.

According to Poulantzas, economic interests divide the bourgeoisie. Capitalists compete with each other: this is their economic relation. They cannot overcome this competition on their own and thus they are unable to act collectively.[52] While reproduction of capitalism is in the collective interest of the bourgeoisie, it is not in the interest of individual capitalists: without relying on the rational choice framework, Poulantzas understood that capitalists face a free rider problem.[53] Moreover, reproduction of capitalism, particularly in the face of political threat from the working class, requires economic sacrifices on the part of capitalists and, again, it is not in the interest of individual capitalists to make these sacrifices. Hence, the task of reproducing capitalism cannot be assumed by the bourgeoisie; it can be accomplished only by the state acting against objections of individual firms. To maintain capitalism the state must be independent from the influence of capitalists: this is Poulantzas' theory of the relative autonomy of state.

The haunting question again is why the state that is autonomous from capitalists would invariably act to reproduce capitalism. Poulantzas is convinced that the autonomous state must indeed perform its function of reproducing capitalism: it is for this reason that the autonomy of state is "relative." He relies on several explanations. At times he cites structural limitations of state institutions under capitalism; at other times he argues that reproduction of capitalism is in the self-interest of the state apparatus. In the end he seems to conclude that the state reproduces capitalism because no political force that can organize collectively under this system would want the state to do anything else or, conversely, because only those political forces that would want the state to reproduce capitalism can organize under this system: I am not sure.

According to Poulantzas, the manner in which classes become organized politically under capitalism is an effect of state actions.[54] In particular, workers do not appear organized as a class in politics just because of the position they share within the system of production. Poulantzas' treatment of the working class is truly convoluted: the potential revolutionary threat emanating from the working class is what drives the state, yet the working class never appears as an actor threatening capitalism. He takes it as axiomatic that workers are revolutionary; he seeks to explain why they do not appear as such in history. Needless to say, empirical consequences of this theory are not easy to find: everything happens because of the potential threat by the working class but the state prevents the working class from realizing this potential. In fact, the state even prevents the working class from organizing collectively as a revolutionary force.

Workers are first a category defined within the system of production. Yet capitalism individualizes class relations. Capitalism is a system in which relations between persons and things ("property") are distinguished from relations between persons ("contract"). Both of these relations are universalistic and egalitarian. Under capitalism, law and ideology treat all property in the same way, thus obscuring the distinction, between productive assets and articles of consumption, which defines class relations. Under capitalism, law and ideology treat all contract partners in the same way, as "individuals," thus obscuring the fact that workers, who cannot survive without selling their capacity to work, are compelled to enter into employment contracts. [Balibar, 1970] Finally, according to Poulantzas, capitalist political institutions treat everyone as abstract "citizens," without identifying them by the places they occupy in the class relation as capitalists and workers. In this sense, capitalism disorganizers workers as a class: while their common class interest opposes them, as workers, to capitalism, they appear as "individuals-citizens," rather than as workers, within capitalist law, ideology and politics.[55]

But even if workers appear in the realm of politics as individuals-citizens, could not they still organize politically against capitalism? Poulantzas' answer, which follows very closely that of Gramsci [1971], is that in contemporary capitalism the state assures that workers would not be ready to act against this system. Here the function of the state is to organize class compromise: the contemporary capitalist state is a "popular class state." The state forces the bourgeoisie to pay the economic cost for their political interest in preserving capitalism. Like Gramsci, Poulantzas is not quite clear whether the mechanism by which the working class is co-opted into capitalism consists of concessions or of a free competition within some institutionally defined limits. In principle, the "popular class state" can be a dictatorship which measures concessions necessary to mobilize the consent of the working class or a democracy where working class parties struggle to improve material conditions of workers.

Ultimately, the central question remains unanswered: why would the state function to regulate capitalism, why would it reproduce capitalism against capitalists, why would it disorganize the revolutionary threat from the working class? For Poulantzas, capitalism cannot last unless the state assures that different socially organized activities are functional for capitalist production, unless it coerces the particularistic bourgeoisie into defense of its collective interest, and unless it prevents the organization of the working class as a revolutionary actor. And the state invariably does all this. While the Offe — Habermas theory at least allows the state to fail in its tasks, Poulantzas' capitalism is impregnable unless someone, somehow, destroys the state altogether.

2.4. State theories of reproduction: a critique

The overall structure of marxist theories of the state is the following. Some conditions must be fulfilled if capitalism is to last. For one reason or another these conditions are not created spontaneously by the capitalist system of production and exchange. Therefore, if capitalism survives, it must be because the state provides these conditions by performing some specific functions.

Accumulation and social peace are the two general conditions of reproduction of capitalism. Each of them calls, in turn, for more specific conditions. Accumulation will take place if and only if investment is profitable, if competition is sufficiently vigorous to assure that the rate of profit is positive in all sectors, if investments which are either too large or unprofitable for particular firms and necessary for all are undertaken by the state, if commodities are exchanged on markets rather than distributed according to other criteria. Moreover, accumulation requires some definite non-economic conditions to be present. Social peace or legitimacy call for conditions of their own.

The capitalist system of production and exchange cannot generate all of these conditions necessary for its continued existence, for a number of reasons:

(1) The reason cited most generally is the falling profitability. Some writers, including Poulantzas [1973], rely on Marx's law of the falling

rate of profit. Others, notably Hirsch [1978], see the threat to profits in wage pressure. Whatever the reason and in spite of conceptual and measurement problems, it seems that indeed the pre-tax rate of profit has had a downward secular trend in all capitalist countries. Insufficient profitability constitutes a threat to capitalist reproduction which is logically obvious and empirically robust.

(2) Withdrawal of commodities from the realm of circulation, considered by Offe as a pre-condition for capitalist production, in particular, the growth of compulsory education, pension systems, mass armies, family allowances and other barriers to entry to the labor market, reduces the supply of labor and allows wages to exceed the level of subsistence. The "surplus population," even if available in excess of the demand for labor, does not function as a "reserve army of the unemployed".

(3) The transformation of capitalism from a competitive to "corporate," "organized," "monopoly," "late" or otherwise non-competitive phase — the cornerstone of several theories — is alleged to have destroyed the capacity of the market to reproduce itself. We are told by Habermas that under "late" capitalism "the law of value no longer operates" but neither why nor with what consequences. And there are good reasons to think that the entire emphasis is misplaced: even if it is true that capital became concentrated, it need not follow that capitalism becomes less competitive. Indeed, as Clifton [1978] argued, modern giant corporations can move capital and contest markets at a scale impossible for Marx's family firms. Finally, an empirical study by Semmler [1985] failed to find evidence of widespread non-competitive pricing. Altogether, the obsession with periodization often serves as a cover for a theoretical laziness: instead of specifying which conditions for reproduction have disappeared in the course of history of capitalism, all we get are labels.

(4) Several writers emphasize that even some economic conditions of capitalist production are not recreated by the market. According to O'Connor [1973], as a result of the increasing socialization of production, the scale of infrastructural investments required for continued capitalist production surpassed the capacity of single firms. Altvater [1978: p. 41] pointed out that the market will not generate sufficient quantities of public goods: "Not all social functions can be organized in a capitalist way, either because the production of material infra-

structure does not promise any profit or because the required conditions are so general and comprehensive that they cannot profitably be realized by individual units of capital. . . . Capital cannot of itself, through it own action, produce the social preconditions of its existence.''

(5) Altvater's last sentence goes beyond economic conditions. In Hirsch's [1978: p. 66] formulation, ''the capitalist process of reproduction structurally presupposes social functions which cannot be fulfilled by individual capitals.'' As we have seen, Poulantzas agreed. The list of such functions would be long.

(6) Finally, capitalism is threatened by the working class. All marxist writers take it as axiomatic that interests of workers and capitalists are irrevocably opposed: indeed, they say nothing about interests of workers, treating them as but a zero-sum complement to the interests of capitalists. Since capitalists want to preserve capitalism, workers must want to abolish it.

Faced with these functional problems, the capitalist system of production and exchange cannot recreate the conditions of its own existence. Thus if capitalism is still around, it must be because these conditions are produced by the state. At this moment, it is necessary to reflect on the structure of these theories. They invoke the role of the state to explain why capitalism has survived various threats to its existence. To this extent, these are ''state theories of reproduction of capitalism,'' rather than theories of the state. Indeed, all that these theories have to say about the state and its actions is derived by inference from the conditions that must have been fulfilled and from actions that would have fulfilled them given that capitalism had survived a particular threat. States do all that is necessary for capitalist reproduction and only that which is necessary for reproduction. Hence, these theories imply hypotheses of the following form: given that these specific conditions must be fulfilled if capitalism is to survive a particular functional disturbance and given that any one of the following policies fulfills this condition, since capitalism had survived this disturbance, the state must have pursued one of these policies. One should expect, therefore, a relation between particular threats to capitalism and specific public policies.

Statistical work based on these theories is very limited: the favorite
method of scholars in this tradition was to illustrate theories in case
studies that cast little light on their empirical validity. Statistical
evidence that does exist strongly supports the central hypothesis. For
example, Griffin et al. [1982: p. 354] concluded one of their exceptionally careful econometric analyses of the United States as follows: "We
believe the results presented in this paper demonstrate that welfare
expenditure policy is one vehicle used by state managers in the US as
they try to insure capital accumulation, to placate or encourage
competing class groups, and to acquiesce to or rebuff demands of mass
insurgents, all within the context of tenuously legitimate electoral
institutions."

Unfortunately, even such conclusions would not be sufficient to
establish the empirical validity of these theories. Marxist theories of the
state relate threats to specific requirements of capitalist reproduction
— "functional gaps" — to specific interventions by the state. But this
theoretical program runs into an insurmountable obstacle: as the
capital-logic debate has shown, no-one knows how to ascertain ex ante
what it is that capitalism requires in the specific place at a particular
time. Take profitability: everyone would agree that investment must be
profitable if accumulation is to occur. But why is investment insufficiently profitable, say in France today? Is it because wages are too high?
Payroll taxes are too high? Labor force is insufficiently skilled?
Technology is obsolete? Energy is too costly? Risk is too high, given
foreign competition? There are too many regulations? People do not
want to work any more? Other reasons? Conversely, any policy that
would lower wages, reduce payroll taxes, improve vocational education, increase research, increase protection from foreign competition,
decrease costs of energy, reduce environmental costs or increase labor
time may do the trick of increasing profitability and thus perhaps
stimulating accumulation. The very fact that any particular functional
need of capitalism can, under any concrete conditions, be fulfilled by a
variety of state actions renders marxist theories of the state predictively
impotent.[56] Indeed, one striking aspect of the various theories is that
while they differ in diagnosing the threat to reproduction, they end up
with almost identical lists of functions that the state must perform.
These functions seem to be identified ex post: whatever states do must
be their function. This is why conclusions such as those of Griffin et al.
do not rehabilitate the theory: even if it is true that welfare expendi-

tures in the United States were used by state managers to reproduce capitalism, why were welfare expenditures and not other policies used to reproduce capitalism? It would be illusive to believe that under capitalism in general or in the United States in particular state managers must deal with popular demands by expanding the welfare state. The optimistic faith that capitalist states achieve social peace only by legitimation allowed the Left to be stunned by the neo-liberal revolution. One cannot deduce state policies from requirements of capitalist reproduction.

Ultimately, marxist theories of the state failed to establish their central hypothesis, namely, that capitalism is still around only because it is supported by actions of state institutions [Gernsteberger, 1978]. For all we know, the capitalist system may be so resilient that it can tolerate all the functional gaps. Certainly, we have not seen a case of capitalism crumbling because the state failed to fulfill its functions, and most people would probably agree that we have seen states fail. Reagan's victory dealt a fatal blow to state theories of reproduction. Neo-liberals compaigned to reduce state intervention, to deregulate, to lower protection, to suppress unions, to dismantle the welfare state; in sum to let the market to itself. And marxist theoreticians kept asserting that capitalists do not understand the functional requirements of reproduction of capitalism; that capitalism cannot exist without planning, without systematic state intervention [Wolfe, 1981]. Capitalism "cannot go back": this was the comforting conclusion of marxist theories of the state. And yet, repression of unions, reduction of the welfare system, privatization of the public sector and abatement of regulation look increasingly like a credible, and ominous, alternative for the future of capitalism [Przeworski and Wallerstein, 1982b].

Since this weakness is fatal, it would be gratuitous to delve into detailed criticisms. Yet two additional difficulties faced by these theories merit attention, since they define issues of a broader interest. First, how does the state acquire its capacity to function? Secondly, what is the role of class struggle in shaping public policies?

The first point received attention from several critics, notably Skocpol [1980, 1985]. Clearly, in order to be able to perform the tasks necessary to reproduce capitalism under particular historical circumstances, state institutions must have specific technical capacities. State managers must know what is necessary for accumulation and legitimacy [Wirth, 1975]; the state must have an extensive information gathering bureaucracy; state managers must have a technical theory that would guide state interventions.[57] To collect income taxes one needs an immense bureaucracy, with buildings, desks, machines: a government cannot overnight decide to collect income taxes even if it is vital for reproduction of capitalism. Thus, in Skocpol's analysis, state institutions in the United States in 1929 were just incapable of pursuing policies that would save capitalism. Indeed, Poulantzas' theory is even logically inconsistent: if instances are relatively autonomous and develop unevenly, what guarantees that the state would be always developed appropriately to perform its functions?

In fact, the state as an institution is never present in these functionalist analyses. Since, by assumption, the state invariably responds to the functional requirements of capitalist reproduction and since its policies have, by assumption, the function of fulfilling these requirements, one can proceed from requirements to reproduction without bothering with the state at all. The very concept of the state is based on a reification. The state is ready-to-wear; it is always in its functional garb before anything threatens the reproduction of capitalist relations.

Finally, the perennial difficulty of any functionalist perspective is to account for the reasons why conflicts among specific groups under concrete historical circumstances would always, or at least "regularly," "normally," "most of the time," result in states performing their functions. It is true that once the manner in which a society responds to variations of historical conditions had been institutionalized, much of this response is automatic. Yet it is equally apparent that activities of institutions and these institutions themselves are a continual outcome of conflicts. Under concrete conditions, particular groups enter into conflicts over particular issues, and the outcome of these conflicts is a particular form of organization and a specific set of policies. What is not clear is why these policies would predictably have the function of reproducing capitalist relations. Clearly, the answer to this question cannot be that the state reproduces capitalist because this "is" its function. This answer can be twofold: either the capitalist system is organized in such a manner that it is reproduced in spite of all conflicts, and then these conflicts, including class conflicts, acquire the status of a superfluous ritual, or outcomes of conflicts do in fact determine the policies that states pursue, in which case the burden of explanation is shifted to these conflicts and any concept of function becomes redundant.

3. CLASS CONFLICT AND THE STATE

Why then do states do what they do? Specifically, why do they act in the interest of capitalism or capitalists? Three answers emerged in marxist debates: (1) the "power elite" theory asserts that governments act on behalf of capitalists because state managers have the same interests or values as capitalists, (2) the "selectiveness" theory claims that there is something about the organizational structure of all state institutions under capitalism which renders governments incapable of making certain decisions, and (3) the "structural dependence" theory maintains that the private ownership of productive assets imposes constraints which no government and no policy can override.

Among these answers, the "selectiveness" theory is the least developed and the least convincing. Its main claim is that several issues, in particular those crucial to class interests, never become subject matter of political discussion and governmental activity in capitalist societies [Bachrach and Baratz, 1970]. The key to the class character of capitalist states is thus to be found in "non-decisions" and the explanation for this inaction on specific issues is located in the organizational structure of states. The empirical problems confronting a theory of this nature are formidable [Offe, 1974] and, perhaps as the result, little progress has occurred along such lines. Hence, I will not consider this theory below. In turn, the power elite theory is the subject of Section 3.1. while the structural dependence theory is discussed in Section 3.2.

3.1. Power elite theory

While several versions of this theory have been put forth [Mills, 1956, Domhoff, 1970], Miliband's [1969] version is the most complete and systematic. Miliband argues that governments act in the interest of capitalism because capitalists control state institutions and use them as instruments for the realization of their interests.

Miliband observes first that capitalist societies are characterized by inequality. In all capitalist societies a small group owns a large share of wealth and derives various privileges from that ownership. He then proceeds to demonstrate that these same people — people who are wealthy, who attend the same elite schools, and share the same values — populate the state apparatus as appointed officials, judges and elected politicians. Thus, the conclusion is that capitalist societies are governed by one "ruling class": economic elites add up to a "dominant class" and the dominant class is the same as the "state elite." "What the evidence conclusively suggests," Miliband maintains, "is that in terms of social origin, education and class situation, the men who have manned *all* command positions in the state system have largely, and in many cases overwhelmingly, been drawn from the world of business and property, or from the professional middle classes." [1969: p. 66]

While this argument is buttressed by an impressive medley of facts, Miliband is aware that it raises a number of puzzles. If capitalist states are almost invariably controlled by capitalists, what is the role of political competition, specifically of elections? Miliband responds by offering two, somewhat contradictory, arguments that political competition under capitalism is always unequal.

The first argument goes back to Marx and was used by Lenin to qualify capitalist democracy as a "dictatorship of the bourgeoisie": "formal equality" cannot override "real inequality." Suppose that political competition is perfectly universalistic, equal, and fair: the same rules apply to everyone, in an equal manner and are blindly enforced. Yet the ownership of wealth endows capitalists with a number of resources which give them advantage in elections. Money matters because campaigns are costly. Wealthy people have more time to spend on politics. People who organize production have ready-made organizational skills which they can apply to politics. Thus, the resources with which classes enter into electoral politics are unequal and when unequal parties confront each other in a formally equal competition those who enter with greater resources invariably win. Just think of a perfectly refereed football game in which players on one team outweigh the other team by 50 pounds each! Wealthy people win fair elections and use their victories to perpetuate their wealth.

The second argument is superfluous given the first one and, once introduced, it ends up having a subversive effect. The additional reason why the dominant class wins elections is that formal rules of competition are biased in its favor. But Miliband does not notice that if institutions are not epiphenomenal, if they have autonomous causal power, then they could be used to overcome economic inequality, not only to reinforce it. Political institutions could be designed in such a way as to compensate for the lack of resources: campaigns can be publicly financed, access to media can be given freely, etc.

According to Miliband, political competition repeatedly returns the ruling class to office. But there are some exceptions: sometimes the Left does win elections and forms governments. Miliband's explanation why tenure in office by socialist parties does not undermine the ruling class thesis relies on traditional arguments about the co-optation of working-class leaders, prominent already in his first book, *Parliamentary Socialism* [1972 (1961)]. Miliband sees these leaders as confronting a radical choice: either they dedicate their efforts to abolishing capitalism or succumb to the power of capital [1969: p. 152]. Given this choice, they invariably give up.

Hence even when electoral competition does not bring the members of the ruling class into office, governments still continue to act in the interest of this class, which for Miliband implies that they act against the interest of the subordinated masses. The final puzzle is why would those who lose constantly because the ruling class controls the state consent to their rule? Miliband's answer relies on "ideological domination." The ownership of means of production extends to the means of intellectual production and these are used to persuade people to hold beliefs contrary to their interests.[58] The ruling class puts wool over the eyes of the subordinated masses.

This entire argument is so strained that, despite the rich empirical support, Miliband's central thesis is unpersuasive. Moreover, the weakest point in this argument was not anticipated by Miliband but raised by Poulantzas [1972]. Miliband's argument assumes that capitalists are capable of coordinating their interests in such a way that the state could act on behalf of one, coherent and consistent, "interest of the capitalist class." As many others, Miliband [1969: p. 5] followed Marx's claim from the *Communist Manifesto* that "The executive of the modern state is but a committee for managing the common affairs of the whole bourgeoisie." But what are the *common* affairs of the *entire* bourgeoisie? These cannot be the affairs that place individual capitalists in competition with one another. They could entail either those interests that pit the bourgeoisie as a class against other classes or those interests that concern the viability of capitalism as a system. But even those interests, as collective interests, give rise to free-rider problems and intra-capitalist conflicts. In particular, the survival of capitalism may be possible only at the cost of particular capitalists and may not be in their individual interest. The interest of "capitalism" and of "capitalists" is not the same: the survival of capitalism is not in the interest of individual capitalists[59]. Hence, to cite Offe [1974: p. 34], "we cannot take a coherent and consistent class consciousness of the ruling class as a starting-point for a reconstruction of the class character of the state activity — even if we assume the influence theory argumentation to be correct empirically."

3.2. Structural dependence theory

While elite theory assumes that state managers adopt the same objectives as capitalists, structural dependence theory asserts that the private ownership of productive assets imposes constraints which are so binding that no government, regardless what its objectives might be, can pursue policies adverse to interests of capitalists. A summary of this theory has been put forth by Offe: "In a policy making process in which the state solves *its own* problems . . . those groups are strategically located which are in a position to obstruct successful policies. This is, under capitalist relationships of production, the class of owners of (money) capital. What this class basically does is to decide on the volume, place, time and kind of exchange processes to take place. Seen in this way, the political power of the capitalist class does not reside in what its members do politically (exert "power" and "influence" in the decision making process, etc.) but it resides rather in what its members can *refuse to do economically* (namely initiate exchange processes through buying labor power and fixed capital), i.e. *invest*." [1975b: p. 9]

This theory begins with the hypothesis that the entire society depends on the allocation of resources chosen by owners of capital. Investment decisions have public and long lasting consequences: they determine the future possibilities of production, employment, and consumption for all. Yet they are private decisions. Since every individual and group must consider their future, since future consumption possibilities depend on present investment and since investment decisions are private, all social groups are constrained in the pursuit of their material interests by the effect of their actions on the willingness of owners of capital to invest, which in turn depends on the profitability of investment. In a capitalist society, the trade-off between present and future consumption for all passes through a trade-off between consumption of those who don't own capital and profits.

Consider this dependence from the point of view of one group, wage-earners. At any instant of time, wages and profits are indeed inversely related as Marx argued in *Wage Labour and Capital* [1952a]. In a world without a future, wage-earners would be best off consuming the entire product, indeed confiscating the capital stock. But wage-earners care about their future as well as present income and future wages depend on private investment. If firms respond to wage increases with less investment, wage-earners may be best off moderating their wage demands. Workers' future income depends upon the realization of capitalists' present interests.

While the theory is usually stated with regard to workers' wage demands, to the extent that material means are required to advance their welfare, structural dependence binds all groups: minorities struggling for economic equality, women wanting to transform the division of labor within the household, old people searching for material security, workers striving for safer working conditions or the military seeking bombs. It is in this sense that capitalism is a class society: not in the sense that there are always two organized classes, but in the sense that the structure of property characteristic of capitalism makes everyone's material conditions dependent upon the private decisions of owners of wealth.

The theory of structural dependence continues with the inference that since the entire society depends on the owners of capital, so must the state. Whether particular governments have interests and goals of their own or they act on behalf of a coalition of groups or a class, the pursuit of any objectives that require material resources places governments in the situation of structural dependence. Politicians seeking re-election must anticipate the impact of their policies on the decisions of firms because these decisions affect employment, inflation, and personal income of voters: vote-seeking politicians are dependent on owners of capital because voters are. Even a government which was a perfect agent of wage-earners could not and would not behave much differently from one that represents capitalists. If workers are best off with a fair dose of wage restraint, a pro-labor government will also avoid policies that dramatically alter the distribution of income and wealth. The range of actions which governments find best for the interests they represent is narrowly circumscribed whatever these interests may be.

The reason the state is structurally dependent is that no government can simultaneously reduce profits and increase investment. Firms invest as a function of expected returns; policies which transfer income away from owners of capital reduce the rate of return and thus of investment. Governments face a trade-off between distribution and growth, between equality and efficiency. They can trade a more (or less) egalitarian distribution of income for less (or more) investment but they cannot alter the terms of this trade-off: this is the central thesis of the theory of structural dependence. Governments can and do choose between growth and income distribution but because material welfare of any constituency depends upon economic growth as well as its share of income and because distribution can be achieved only at the cost of growth, all governments end up pursuing policies with limited redistributive effects.[60]

The belief that under capitalism governments are structurally dependent on capital is widespread. Miliband [1969: p. 152] portrayed this dependence as follows: "given the degree of economic power which rests in the 'business community' and the decisive importance of its actions (or its non-actions) for major aspects of economic policy, any government with serious pretensions to radical reform must either seek to appropriate that power or find its room for radical action rigidly circumscribed by the requirements of 'business confidence'." Block [1977: p. 15] maintained that "In a capitalist economy the level of economic activity is largely determined by private investment decisions of capitalists. This means that capitalists, in their collective role as investors, have a veto over state policies in that their failure to invest at adequate levels can create major political problems for state managers." Lindblom [1977: p. 172 and p. 175] observed that "Because public functions in the market system rest in the hands of businessmen, it follows that jobs, prices, production, growth, the standard of living, and the economic security of everyone all rest in their hands. . . . In the eyes of government officials, therefore, businessmen do not appear simply as representatives of special interest. . . . They appear as functionaires performing functions that government officials regard as indispensable."

Przeworski and Wallerstein [1988] examined the validity of this theory considering whether governments can redistribute income to wage-earners without causing a fall of investment in a linear production world in which firms choose the rate of investment to maximize the present value of the utility their stockholders derive from consumptions, while unions, where they can, do the same for their members by choosing the labor share of value added (or the wage rate, given that employment is determined by the capital stock). They have shown that without the government, wage-earners are structurally dependent on capital, in the sense that all increases in wages occur, dollar for dollar, at the cost of investment. The same turns out to be true when a government distributes income to wage-earners by imposing a tax on incomes from property. Yet the result no longer holds when a government taxes only the uninvested profits and transfers this revenue to wage-earaners. Indeed, with a pure tax on uninvested profits and a powerful union willing to trade private wages for transfers and government services, a pro-labor government can cause any distribution of income it desires and increase investment. Moreover, contrary to widespread beliefs, as long as governments are administratively capable of taxing capital outflows, international mobility of capital does not affect this result, even when governments compete for investment [Wallerstein, 1988]. The conclusion, then, is that under capitalism governments do have a choice of economic policies and these policies have consequences: the structural dependence theory is false.

It bears repeating that structural dependence refers to the constraints imposed on governments by decentralized, narrowly economic actions of particular firms. What these results deny, therefore, is only the hypothesis, to use a clear formulation by Block [1977: p. 19], "that conspiracies to destabilize the regime are basically superfluous, since decisions made by individual capitalists according to their narrow economic rationality are sufficient to paralyze the regime, creating a situation where the regime's fall is the only possibility."

Even this narrow result, moreover, is subject to a number of caveats. While the conclusion does not depend on the linear production function, it is sensitive to the utility function of capitalists. In particular, if capitalists care about absolute levels of consumption independently of present and future profits, the result may no longer hold. Even more importantly, if capital is internationally mobile, anticipations that governments would introduce such policies may cause a fall in investment and thus impose a cost on wage-earners. Hence, the state may be structurally dependent in the dynamic sense that, given the cost of anticipations, left-wing governments may best promote the interests of their constituencies by assuring capitalists that they would not pursue such policies.

Although these results are inconclusive, they do cast doubt on the validity of the structural dependence theory. They suggest that economic trade-offs may be not as binding as marxist theoreticians and leftist politicians seem to believe. At the same time, they direct out attention to non-economic, institutional and ideological, constraints.

4. CONCLUSIONS

Some basic facts are generally accepted. The role of the state vis-a-vis the economy had increased dramatically since World War I, at least until the late 1970s and at least among the OECD countries. A number of reforms improved the conditions of work and of life of workers and other wage-earners. The bourgeoisie, or at least important groups of capitalists, at many time opposed reforms and assumed generally anti-statist positions. Yet two conflicting views of the relation between states and capitalists economies continue to persist.

Anticipated already in 1910 by Hilferding's notion of "organized capitalism," functionalist marxism saw the key to the longevity of capitalism in interventions by the state. Convinced that markets are inevitably chaotic, this perspective discovered in the state the architect of economic order. These two deeply held beliefs — the doubt that decentralized actions could provide a foundation of a social order and the faith in the capacity of the state as the demiurge of society — delimited the problematic of functionalist marxism.[61]

A period of exceptionally intense productivity having been experienced, this approach ran out of steam because it repeatedly failed to sustain its central hypothesis, namely, that capitalism survives only because of state intervention. It also failed to resolve a number of logical and political problems that strained the credibility of the theory. The main embarrassment for this approach is class conflict.

On the one hand, the existence of massive union and political movements of workers and the reforms forged by these movements constantly tore the logical seams of the theory. The resolution, suggested already by Poulantzas [1973] and proposed explicitly by Muller and Neussus [1975] and by Block [1977] was torturous. Block admitted class conflict among the capitalist class, managers of the state apparatus, and the working class. Yet the net effect of this conflict is only to rationalize capitalism: "Pressures from the working class have contributed to the expansion of the state's role in the regulation of the economy and in the provision of services. . . . The capacity of the state to impose greater rationality on capitalism is extended into new areas as a result of working-class pressures" [1977: p. 22]. Hence, in the end, the working class turns out to be an accomplice in reproducing capitalism and it is always an unwitting one. Workers never appear within this framework as subjects: they are either victims of repression, dupes of ideological domination or casualties of betrayal by leaders.

On the other hand, the functionalist approach is equally ill at ease when confronting repeated instances when the bourgeoisie or at least major groups thereof appear anti-statist. If the state always strengthens capitalism and if the viability of capitalism is in the interest of capitalists, why would any bourgeoisie be ever anti-statist? Obviously, one answer is that capitalism is a public good; hence, it is not in the interest of individual capitalists to pay costs for its reproduction. A tack adopted more frequently is to speak of "fractions," which have conflicting interests. But the one possibility this approach cannot admit is that individual capitalists or their organizations turn anti-statist simply because the state threatens their interests, regardless whether that has anything to do with reproducing capitalism. If the state is run by the ruling class, the very possibility that state managers would pursue policies that hurt capitalists as a class is precluded.

Thus, while several problems — an implausible account of capitalism, the inability to explain why governments pursue particular policies, the reification of the state — plague the functionalist perspective, this perspective is made necessary by an incorrect model of class conflict in democratic capitalist societies. The very problem of reproduction appears as a functional one because the model of irreconcilable class conflict leads to the conclusion that capitalism could not have survived as an outcome of spontaneous strategic interactions among wage-earners, firms, and governments.

Once agents and their actions are taken seriously, the notion that the state under capitalism performs any kind of "functions" becomes untenable. Policies of particular governments, their economic and political effects, and their consequences for the viability of capitalism are then analyzed as contingent outcomes of strategic interactions among multiple political forces the interests of which involve varying mixes of conflict and cooperation.

Although class conflict was introduced into marxist theories of the state by Poulantzas in 1978, marxists resisted the adoption of a technical language for analyzing strategic interactions. Conversely, neo-classical economists, particularly in the United States, until recently shied away from admitting governments and unions as strategic actors that affect economic outcomes. As a result, only in the last few years did strategic analyses of class conflict overcome these resistances. Nevertheless, there are already several bodies of literature which analyze class conflict at various levels of aggregation:

(1) efficient wage models [Schapiro and Stiglitz, 1984; Bowles, 1985] explain why the labor market does not clear in equilibrium by focusing on the conflicts inherent in the labor process;

(2) firm-level collective bargaining models [recent reviews are Oswald, 1985; Malcolmson, 1987] assert that unions and firms will cooperate if agreements about employment (specifically capital/labor ratios) can be enforced;

(3) models of unionization with employer resistance and costly organizing [Lazear, 1983; Wallerstein, 1988] explain why union density varies across industries and countries;

(4) models that focus on union structure [Oswald, 1979; Wallerstein and Przeworski, 1988] lead to the conclusion that large centralized unions are more willing to offer wage restraint if they organize workers who are complements in production;

(5) finally, following the seminar article by Lancaster [1973], several analyses of a dynamic game between one centralized union, choosing the wage rate or the labor share, and many homogeneous firms, choosing investment, point to various sources of inefficiency associated with non-cooperative solutions [Basar, Haurie and Ricci, 1985; Hoel, 1978; Mehrling, 1986; van der Ploeg, 1987; Pohjola, 1983, 1984; Przeworski and Wallerstein, 1982; Schott, 1984].

Nevertheless, models that involve strategic interaction among unions, firms and governments are still relatively scarce. One such model, discussed above, in which governments choose policies anticipating the reactions of strategic unions and firms, was utilized by Przeworski and Wallerstein [1988] to study the structural dependence of the state. Another class of models analyzes the interaction among large unions, decentralized firms and governments with regard to employment [Calmfors and Horn, 1985; Hersoug, 1985; Driffil, 1985;

Soederstroem, 1985; Scharpf, 1988]. The union, anticipating that firms will hire to maximize profits (on the demand for labor curve) and that governments will try to avoid unemployment, pushes its wage up, beyond the level it would have chosen in the absence of accommo-dating governments. Governments find themselves in a situation where the optimal strategy is not consistent: the optimal strategy is not to accommodate, the consistent strategy is to expand demand once union wages threaten to create unemployment in the private sector. To obtain the result that strong unions cause inflation or balance of payment difficulties those models must rely, however, on some less than general assumptions: either that the union does not internalize the costs of inflation it generates or that the union is myopic or that it has some public sector employment targets different from the government or some other contrivance.

The class-conflict approach suffers thus far from a number of limitations. Firms appear only as individual actors and are almost always on their best response with regard to employment or investment.[62] Government objectives appear difficult to model.[63] General equilibrium results with multiple unions and mobile capital are highly indeterminate. Nevertheless, the game-theoretic approach to class relations is still in infancy.

The central issues concerning the relation between the state and the economy within the marxist perspective still remain open. We still do not know the manner and the degree to which the private ownership of productive wealth constrains governments. This is the central question since it has two consequences of political importance. First, if the private ownership of the means of the production is so constraining that no government, regardless of its electoral mandate, can pursue policies directed against interests of capitalists, then democratic institutions are impotent. Secondly, if all governments are structurally constrained, including military dictatorships, then the bourgeoisie has nothing to fear from abdicating from direct political participation and entrusting their interest to autonomous state institutions. But if the economic power of individual firms is not sufficiently binding to constrain all governments, then the outcomes of the democratic process do matter for the welfare of particular groups and the bourgeoisie has reasons to mistrust the state and to fear state autonomy.

If economic constraints are not as binding as marxist theoreticians traditionally believed, then it becomes even more puzzling why left-wing governments either cause relatively little difference when they are in office or fail miserably when they try to make more of a difference. One explanation would return to the political orgnization of capitalists: at least when threatened by left-wing governments, capitalists are able to organize collectively to defend their interests by political actions. Another explanation would return to the institutional considerations: governments operate not only under constraints of private economy but also — something we tend to miss — under the constraint of states understood as organizational structures. As a result, states as institutions are unresponsive to expressions of popular preferences in elections. Indeed, the dilemma of the Left is that any improvement of the welfare of wage-earners requires the intervention of the state but states are blunt instruments of intervention. Finally, even when discussing the economy, we must not neglect ideological factors. Left-wing governments often come to office determined to demonstrate to their opponents that they, too, can responsibly administer capitalitalist economies. The economic, political, institu-tional and ideological explanations of the impregnability of capitalism constitute rival hypotheses. We still do not know enough to eliminate any one among them.

Part IV: Conclusions

None among the arguments reviewed here is conclusive. Theories which maintain that governments respond to preferences of individuals expressed through elections are credible only under most restrictive conditions. The proof that the same individual preferences can in general be aggregated as different collective outcomes deprives these theories of predictive power. Theories which hold that states do what their managers want, whether in the "state-centric" version or in models of autonomous bureaus, fail to establish that state autonomy is inevitable. At the macro-historical level, state autonomy seems to depend on group conflicts, while the autonomy of bureaus under democracy is highly sensitive to detailed institutional arrangements. Finally, theories which claim that private ownership of productive wealth restricts all governments to such an extent that none can act against interests of capital find it difficult to specify the mechanisms by which this constraint bites.

Since each of these theories contains a grain of truth, it is tempting to adopt an eclectic stance. Yet the role of theories is to eliminate arguments that have a prima facie plausibility through a logical and empirical analysis. Unfortunately, the relative validity of these approaches is difficult to assess, in particular since very few studies explicitly test rival hypotheses. A striking feature of this literature is the paucity of statistical studies that would evaluate the relative contribution of individual preferences, state autonomy and property constraints.

The discussion about the state and the economy, however, is not only academic. The proper role of the state with regard to the economy constitutes the central issue of contemporary political debates. The question whether governments or private property is the main source of irrationality and injustice continues to receive conflicting answers.

Several theories discussed here constitute arguments in political debates. Yet none succeeds to persuade. The democratic process certainly suffers from many imperfections but the neo-liberal conclusion — that the market is superior as the institution through which people express their sovereignty — is theoretically deficient. The fear of autonomous state — the military or the bureaucracy — is well grounded in the contemporary experience. Yet both the state-centric approach and the emphasis on bureaucracy are so programmatic that they prefer to horrify us with omnipresent demons rather than offer an analytical apparatus for distinguishing concrete situations. Finally, there are good historical bases for the presumption that private property of the instruments of production severely limits the freedom of societies to allocate resources. Yet marxists cannot tell a story which would leave at least some room for democracy to affect outcomes within those limits.

Political conflicts involve interests and are not resolved by theoretical arguments. Nevertheless, this review highlights some political traps that might be avoidable.

A perhaps obvious trap is to suppose that because one limitation of democracy is onerous others must be taken more lightly. Even if private property is the most binding constraint on democracy under capitalism, the threats originating from state autonomy and from the limitations of the electoral process are nevertheless real. Imperfections of the political process, autonomy of state institutions and private ownership of productive resources all constitute potential threats to democracy. One trap is to fall into a defence of state intervention in the economy at any cost, even at the cost of autonomous and inefficient state institutions.

The other trap is to dismiss limitations originating from private property altogether. The standard argument runs as follows: (1) The "class nature" of the capitalist state is not a given, (2) The Left has traditionally underestimated, if not ignored, the importance of democracy, therefore (3) The real limitations of popular sovereignty lie in the imperfections of the democratic process. Once the importance of democracy is discovered, we return unhampered to the eighteenth century. The conclusion, about which there would be little controversy, is that "it is unlikely that a non-liberal state would be able to assure a correct functioning of democracy and, on the other hand, it is unlikely that a non-democratic state would guarantee the fundamental liberties" [Bobbio, 1984: p. 7]. The panacea is "democratic participation."

Yet this position is much too facile, for a central question that is ignored is whether it is likely that citizens would be able to enjoy basic material security in the liberal democratic state. Our daily experience demonstrates that liberty and participation can and do coexist with poverty and oppression. To discuss democracy without considering the economy in which this democracy is to function is an operation worthy of an ostrich. The traditional dilemma facing the Left originated from the eventuality that even a procedurally satisfactory democracy may be insufficient to liquidate poverty and oppression in the face of threats originating from private property. This dilemma is as acute today as ever before.

Every society faces three distinct political problems: how to reveal and aggregate individual preferences, how to keep the specialized political institutions responsible, and how to satisfy democratically chosen objectives in allocating scarce resources. These problems are not reducible to one another: a procedurally perfect democracy in the political realm does not resolve problems due to economic inequality and socialization of productive resources makes even more urgent the tasks of aggregating preferences and of supervising the state apparatus. Full-fledged democracy calls for electoral institutions that are representative, state institutions that are responsible and mechanisms for allocating resources that obey the democratic process, nothing less.

NOTES

1. The restrictions under which this theorem holds are severe and numerous. Van den Doel [1979: pp. 110–111] lists 11 "most important" assumptions and Ordeshook's [1978] list is even longer. Voter preferences are single peaked. Either everyone votes or the distribution of voter preferences is not too distinct from one that is unimodal and symmetric. Party leaders are interested only in maximizing votes, not in policy outcomes per se. Moreover, the entire apparatus was developed with regard to competition between two parties, although a theorem in a similar spirit was recently proved by Greenberg and Weber for a particular case of multi-party competition.
2. Whether it makes a difference that the goal of collecting revenue is to provide public goods or to transfer income is a matter of some controversy. Peltzman [1980], in the general spirit of the Chicago school maintains it makes no difference and all government activities can be treated as transfers of income. Thurow [1971] is among those who think that voting for public goods represents a different situation than voting for transfers.
3. Aumann and Kurz consider this rule a basic ingredient of *democratic* society, rather than a feature of *capitalism*. But democracy does not exclude a rule that would prohibit individuals from destroying some of their endowment or from limiting the use to others with destroying ways. It is the norm of private property that provides this, albeit not unrestricted, right.
4. The reader should not infer from this and other examples that individuals must necessarily be selfish. Hochman and Rodgers [1969] considered a situation in which each voter has preferences over the income of others. Thurow [1971] discussed the possibility that voters have preferences directly over some feature of income distribution. Hamada [1973] applied the median voter apparatus to a case in which individuals prefer those distributions of post-vote income which maximize their view of social welfare. The results are that under the customary restrictions (1) the majority equilibrium exists, (2) it is perfectly egalitarian, but (3) it is unstable.
5. A simple model from which all these results can be derived is one in which individuals most prefer the tax rate which maximizes their utility $U(C, L)$, derived from consumption, $C(i)$, and leisure, where

$$C(i) = (1-t)Y(i) + t\Sigma Y(i)/n = (1-t)Y(i) + tY,$$

and the utility of leisure is independent of consumption. The majority equilibrium is the tax rate most preferred by the median voter:

$$t(M) = [Y(M) - Y]/(dY/dt), 0 \leq t \leq 1,$$

where $t(i)$ is the tax rate most preferred by the voter with income $Y(i)$ and $dY/dt < 0$ is the marginal deadweight loss, that is, the rate at which aggregate income declines as the tax rate increases.
6. Kramer and Snyder [1984] allowed non-linear tax schedules and came to the conclusion that the majority equilibrium, if one exists, is the schedule which is regressive for lower incomes, steeply progressive around the median income, and again regressive at higher incomes, which they claim, adds up to taxing the poor and

the rich in favor of the middle class, in confirmation of Stigler [1970]. I must admit that I do not understand this result and the interpretation which the authors attach to it, partly because I find it difficult to make the distinction between the authors nominal tax rates, effective tax rates, and effective net transfer rates.

There are other models which seek to determine tax/transfer outcomes under majority rule but which do not rely on the median voter apparatus. Aumann and Kurz [1977] developed a model which differs from those reviewed above in two respects: (1) Any majority can form and any is equally likely, not necessarily of people with incomes equal and lower than the median income, and (2) Tax rates need not be uniform, that is, different rates may apply to persons with the same income. Moreover, Aumann and Kurz admit a broad variety of tax schedules. They produce two new results: (1) Individual tax rates depend upon utility functions, roughly, upon the degree to which one's utility is sensitive to post-fisc income, with more sensitive individuals paying taxes at a higher rate, and (2) Distribution of individual tax rates depend upon the distribution of "power." Otherwise, a solution always exists; tax schedule may be progressive, regressive, or neutral; there is a negative income tax; and the marginal tax rate (under majority rule) is always between 50 and 100 per cent: results similar to the median voter models.

Finally, Kleiman [1983] analyzed a model in which tax/transfer rates are determined by the fear of revolution and counter-revolution. Even in a plutocracy, the Rich would be willing to redistribute some of their income to prevent a revolution. Similarly, the Poor would be willing to stop short of total redistribution out of the fear that the Rich will seek to establish a plutocracy. Thus an internal solution arises under majority rule without introducing either altruism or deadweight losses.

7. See the bibliography in Romer and Rosenthal [1979]. See also Beck [1978] who has shown in the context of optimal growth that (1) the median rate of time preference is the majority equilibrium among all optimal growth plans, (2) this rate will not be defeated by similar plans which are suboptimal, although (3) it may be defeated by very different suboptimal plans. In other words, the preference of the voter with the median future discount rate would win by majority rule over all other optimal plans allocating resources between consumption and investment in the present and the future.

8. Electoral business cycles would occur when (1) Incumbent governments seek to maximize the chances of their re-election (or an equivalent function of votes), (2) Electoral support is a function of economic conditions, typically, inflation and unemployment, (3) Governments are capable of influencing the relevant economic conditions, and (4) Voters are myopic about the trade-offs among the economic conditions, again typically between inflation and unemployment. The consensus seems to be now that economic fluctuations are not caused by governments seeking votes but there are disagreements as to which of the assumptions is false. The implication of the impossibility theorems is that a stable function relating economic conditions to voting support does not exist, thus rendering moot any efforts to manipulate the economy. The literature on electoral business cycles is immense and it will not be discussed here. [For general reviews see Frey, 1978; Hibbs and Fassbender, 1981; Frey and Schneider, 1982; Alt and Chrystal, 1983; Borooah and Van der Ploeg, 1983; Hibbs, 1987].

9. One might think that inefficiency would emerge independently of the government because of other causes of monopoly. Neo-liberals are armed, however, with estimates by Harberger [1954], according to which the social cost of monopolies is minimal. They consider the perfect market to be a self-reproducing institution. This view contrasts with a neo-liberal program produced recently by the OECD,

according to which "Above all, it has to be recognized that no automatic process exists which guarantees the maintenance of competition." [OECD, 1983a: p. 37] As the result, this program calls for comprehensive government intervention designed to make markets more competitive, while it opposes all other forms of government intervention, trade unions but also concentration of capital.

10. Perhaps because of this neglect of institutions, the objective function which Peltzman imputes to the government is arbitrary. Both in his 1976 and 1980 articles Peltzman has the government maximize "the difference between the number of beneficiaries perceiving the policy as the best deal and losers perceiving it as the worst deal." [1980: p. 222] A policy which maximizes this difference is the "politically dominant policy." The problem is that Peltzman's dominant policy (if one exists, see Section 2.3.) would not win elections under the majority rule: a government maximizing Petlzman's function would lose to a party that maximized votes. Indeed, given in addition that nothing is said about preference configurations, I fail to see any meaning in which Peltzman's policy would be "dominant." Under democracy governments must win elections; under dictatorship they do not. This institutional difference does matter for government objectives.

11. In a recent review of theory and evidence, Saunders and Klau [1985, chapter V] fail to find clear evidence that taxes affect relevant behaviors. They note that "the evidence to date has produced estimates of labour supply responses to taxation which are neither strong nor robust . . ." [p. 166]; that the effect of taxes on the demand for labor is theoretically ambivalent and does not show empirically in a cross-section of the OECD countries [p. 174], that "The view that countries with comparatively high tax burdens tend to be those with weak savings propensities cannot be supported on the basis of the data . . ." [p. 177]; and, finally, that the effect of taxes on investment cannot be assessed in aggregate terms [p. 185].

   Each of these topics is a subject of intense research activities. With regard to the supply of labor, Stuart [1984] reviewed the literature, citing several disparate results, and concluded that in the light of recent studies showing higher responsiveness of women, aggregate income-weighted uncompensated labor elasticity in the United States is around 0.32. Ballard, Shoven, and Whalley [1985] followed the same steps, citing more disparate results, and arrived at the number of 0.15 for the uncompensated elasticity. The same tortuous path led Browning and Johnson [1984] to settle on 0.20 as their central estimate. Each of these articles estimates deadweight losses resulting from the loss of labor supply. Stuart estimates that raising taxes by one dollar would cost between 20.4 and 24.4 cents of income lost because of reduced labor supply; Ballard, Shoven, and Whalley arrive at the estimate of 27.4 cents.

   In general, research results in this area tend to be unstable and the particular calculations are based on more assumptions than Chinese astrology manuals. Thus conclusions are premature. Given the existing evidence, it seems clear, however, that the neo-liberal emphasis on the pernicious effects of taxes is excessive.

12. Another criticism is more obvious, even if controversial. The neo-liberal argument is based on "first best" assumptions: the market with regard to which government causes inefficiency is perfect. Existing markets never are and the question thus becomes whether every government intervention causes a fall of aggregate income in the real world. Peltzman [1976], who provides the most systematic and thorough exposition of the model, does allow that regulation may under some conditions decrease monopoly. This issue has been a subject of polemic between Bhagwati and Tullock.

13. Harberger [1971] defended such comparisons as a means for practical criterion of welfare, assuming that utility is a function of income and by postulating that all units of income should be given equal weight. Under these assumptions welfare loss

(inefficiency) can be measured by the reduction of consumer surplus. That this is not a universally accepted procedure is best shown by this conclusion of a textbook: "attempts to use consumer's surplus to measure welfare losses are largely the application of the inappropriate to measure the undefinable." [Silberberg, 1978: p. 494] For a recent review of controversies on this topic see the article by Morey [1984], entitled "Confuser Surplus."

Browning and Johnson concluded recently [1984] that raising the income of the lowest two quintiles of income distribution by one dollar costs the upper three quintiles $9.51 in disposable incomes. This estimate may or may not be valid but the authors' claim that they are studying the trade-off between equality and efficiency is indefensible. The world in which the rich would have $9.51 more and the poor $1 less may be preferable to the former but not more efficient.

14. A similar point has been made by Joskow and Noll [1981: p. 39] in their review of theories of regulation: "the inherent inefficiencies of regulation that flow from these theories have no natural normative consequence, although one would not deduce this from the tone of the literature. That regulation fails to reach a Pareto optimum is fairly uninteresting if no institutions exist that can reach a point that Pareto-dominates regulation. For regulatory interventions that deal with empirically important market imperfections, the departure of regulatory equilibrium from perfect competition is not normatively compelling."

15. One would think that the exclusive reliance on the market would put economists out of the business of government. But no, both Stigler and Tollison seem to believe that everything would be all right if they could just simply run the economy themselves. Here is Stigler [1975: p. 111]: "This is a thoroughly unattractive role which is assigned to the economist: he does not tell the society what to do in the area of economic policy, but merely draws intricate diagrams to explain why the state undertakes what economic functions it happens to undertake." Tollison [1982: p. 588], speaking of the task of economic theory of politics: "This theory seeks refutable propositions and predictions about how government functions in order to explain the divergences between the prescriptions of economists and governmental practice."

16. This meaning of "relative" should be distinguished from another usage also introduced by Poulantzas [1973]. In the second usage [see in particular Block, 1977], autonomy is relative in the sense that the state has its own objectives but it remains tightly constrained in pursuing these objectives by interests of the economically dominant class. I will use the term "structural dependence of the state on capital" to denote the second meaning. See section 3.

17. For a description of an actual historical process whereby a military dictatorship in Argentina tried to free itself successively from dependence on every external control see O'Donnell, 1977.

18. Elster incorrectly attributes a collectivist bias to Marx's theory of abdication. In Marx's account, it is not "the" bourgeoisie which as a collective actor "abdicates" from power but rather individual capitalists who renounce their political representatives and their very organization as a class. Indeed, Marx [1934: p. 76] refers to the "sheer egoism, which makes the ordinary bourgeois always inclined to sacrifice the general interest of his class for this or that private motive." The mass of the bourgeoisie defects from collective organization and the bourgeoisie dissolves as a class, thus allowing the state to become autonomous: something which the political representatives of the bourgeoisie fail to comprehend. The breakdown of relations of representation within the bourgeoisie as the precipitant of transition to autonomous state was emphasized by Gramsci, 1971.

19. Ironically, Rudolph and Rudolph [1985: p. 45] observed that "Much theory about

state formation in Europe depends on misconceived or historically false contrasts with Asia.''

20. Authors in this tradition seem to take Marx's theory of the state under "normal" conditions as a valid description of the "classical" case. Characteristically, the contrasts are made interchangeably with "classic capitalist pattern" and with "classical theories." Alavi [1972: p. 62], for example, writes "These are conditions which differentiate the post-colonial state fundamentally from the state *as analyzed in classical marxist theory.*" [Italics supplied] O'Donnell [1980: p. 717], as well, contrasts theories about the classic case with historical observations of peripheral countries: "instead of the state being, *as classical theories — i.e. those originating in the center — supposed,* some sort of reflection of civil society, it was, to a large extent on the contrary, the state apparatus that shaped the basic features of our societies." [Italics supplied] But if the state was autonomous with regard to the bourgeoisie in England, France, and Prussia, then the classical case is no longer one of strong bourgeoisie ruling through an instrumental state.

21. Rueschemeyer and Evans [1985: p. 63], having noted that divisions within the dominant class promote state autonomy, discover that "Increased pressure from subordinate classes is a second source of increased state autonomy vis-a-vis the dominant class. Oddly, increasing levels of class conflict probably enhance the state's autonomy vis-a-vis society in general." This is a hypothesis that goes back to Marx.

22. Thus, contrary to Poulantzas [1973], I do not believe that Marx had a theory of state autonomy which did not invoke class balance and, contrary to Elster [1985], I see no distinct "Class balance theory of the state." I must admit, however, that Marx never referred to class balance in his writings contemporaneous to the French events of 1848–1851. The first explanation of Bonaparte's coup d'etat in terms of balance of classes seems to be due to Engels in a text entitled "The real causes of the relative passivity of the French proletariat in December of the last year," *Notes to the People*, 43, London: 21 February 1852. Marx made the first reference to a balance in his final draft, but not the first two drafts, of *The Civil War in France* in 1871.

23. The problem of political organization of the bourgeoisie is by no means trivial, given that firms compete with each other economically. Thus their particularistic interests place them in conflict with one another. Collective organization, in turn, presents the usual free rider considerations. The relationship between the bourgeoisie and the state is discussed in section 3.

24. This power can be contested by the working class, if such a class exists and is organized. It can be also contested by broader and looser groupings, such as the "popular sectors." But it can also be, and in fact often was, contested by landowners. Indeed, in Marx's analyses, the bourgeoisie was often caught fighting on two fronts: still against the aristocracy and already against workers. I do not discuss this aspect of class balance theories: the reader should consult Poulantzas [1973] and Elster [1985].

25. The first statement of this hypothesis was perhaps by Thalheimer in 1930 [1979: pp. 120–121], who contrasted European fascism with Latin America: "Here the military dictatorship, the executive power rendering itself independent, does not emerge from fully developed bourgeois society, from its over-ripeness, from the stress it undergoes when threatened by proletarian revolutions, and from the necessity of entrenching itself against revolution, but rather from the opposite. It emerges from the immaturity of bourgeois development, the numerical and organizational weakness of the bourgeoisie which still faces feudal, land-holding elements that hinder the formation of a strong bourgeois political organization. The army, rather the officer corps, is the strongest and most highly organized political

organization. It exercises the power which the bourgeoisie cannot yet exercise."
26. This theory has been subjected to a scorching conceptual and empirical criticism by Leys [1975], who pointed out that it ignores the British tradition of indirect rule which kept the colonial administration small and the fact that the state grew in most peripheral societies after, and not before, independence. See also Ziemann and Lanzendorfer [1977].
27. This is true not only of Weber or Lane but even of Tilly's essay in Evans, Rueschemeyer, and Skocpol [1985]. This collection of often exceptionally innovative articles remains theoretically heterogeneous in spite of the editor's programmatic intent. Several essays in the volume analyze the autonomy of the state with regard to society while some others, Tilly most notably, offer a perspective that begins with organization of violence by the state. None of this heterogeneity is noticed by Skocpol, whose introductory essay begins the plea for a state-centric approach precisely with a discussion of the concept of autonomy. Given the utter confusion of this essay, I find it particularly arrogant that she would conclude with the admonition that "Rather than become embroiled in a series of abstruse and abstract conceptual debates, let us proceed along the lines of the analytical strategies sketched here." [1985: p. 28]
28. The clearest contrast is provided by Mann [1984: p. 203] for whom "civil society freely gives resources but then loses control and becomes oppressed by the state."
29. This power is perhaps better described as the power to coordinate in the game-theoretic sense of the term, although the purpose of meeting here is to resolve conflicts peacefully.
30. The property rights framework casts the following light on the issue of whether the Soviet party-state apparatus constitutes a "class." Since members of the Soviet elite have no individual property rights to the productive wealth, they are not a "bourgeoisie" in the marxist sense of the term. They do go to jail if they appropriate the surplus of the enterprise they manage. Nevertheless, they do collectively appropriate surplus through the mechanism of oversupplying government activities. Hence, although they have no individual right of benefit, they do have the collective right of usage.
31. These conclusions are derived from the first order conditions of maximization problems set up for each type of state. Citizens of a Republic maximize the fiscal residuum, the managers of a Princedom maximize the fiscal residuum and the taxes and the Bureaucracy maximizes the benefit it derives from government activities.
32. Most of the theories summarized here were produced in democratic capitalist countries and they bear the mark of their origins. Strikingly absent from them is the role of repression, which has been historically massive, and at various moments, particularly in the aftermath of World War I, perhaps decisive in maintaining capitalism. The last marxist theoretician who thought systematically about the relation between capitalism and repression was Gramsci. In the recent writings, only O'Donnell repeatedly raises this problematic.
33. For example, Offe [1975a: p. 6] constructs the problematic of policy analysis as follows. First, he argues that the state must promote accumulation and generate popular support. Then he asserts that "The motive force of all policy formation is the problem of reconciling these elements: policy making of the state is nothing but the process by which these elements are reconciled. . . ."
34. This dating is inevitably arbitrary. Poulantzas' *Political Power and Social Classes in the Capitalist Society* appeared in French in 1968 and a first round of debates between Miliband and Poulantzas appeared in the *New Left Review* in 1969. By 1980 skeptics already had the upper hand and Skocpol's [1980] article constituted a *coup de grace*.

35. For a more extensive discussion of these theories see Carnoy [1984] or Jessop [1982].
36. Balibar [1970] was correct to point out that "simple reproduction," that is, a stationary economy without net investment, is already reproducing its own organization. One could add investment and capitalist consumption to this model without any consequences for reproduction.
37. This exchange is voluntary in the sense that each worker can choose to which capitalists he/she will sell labor services but it is compulsory in the sense that workers cannot survive without selling their labor power to a capitalist.
38. Although he believed that adjustments are not instantaneous and economies undergo various crises, Marx was an equilibrium economist.
39. It is irrelevant here whether the peasant benefits from the protection by the lord; the peasant controls, "owns" in the sense of possession, the conditions of his own existence.
40. This is why capitalism can coexist with different political systems: a feudal democracy is an oxymoron while capitalist economies are compatible with democracy as well as with various forms of dictatorship. Note that this indeterminacy of politics with regard to the capitalist economy is a feature entailed by the capitalist economy, as much as the fact that feudal politics must be based on personal domination is entailed by the feudal economic relations. Hence, in this language, it makes sense to speak of societies, or technically "social formations," as "feudal" or "capitalist," to denote the particular organization of the economy and all those features of politics, ideology or culture that are entailed by it. This is the Althusserian notion of the "determination in the last instance."
41. "Self-reproducing" should not be taken to mean either "unchanging" or "eternal." In Marx's theory, as the social relations of capitalism become reproduced from one cycle of production to another, capitalism develops in a lawful manner. The scale of production increases, the scope of decisions becomes centralized, surplus population grow, and the rate of profit falls. The last two laws of development of capitalism are particularly important for the theory. The growth of the surplus population, which serves as "the reserve army of the unemployed," assures that wages remain at the level of, albeit historically, variable subsistence; that is, that workers do not save out of wages. The falling rate of profit is the source of the mortal threat to capitalism. [See in particular vol. III, pages 253, 259, 264-265].
42. Offe's and Habermas' writings on the state add up to a general theory. Offe's theory is outlined in several articles written principally between 1972 and 1975 and collected in 1984 in *Contradictions of the Welfare State*. Habermas' views of the capitalist state, several of which acknowledge a debt to Offe, were put forth in the *Legitimation Crisis* [1975]. While each author has made distinct contributions and while the emphases differ in some places, their basic views are sufficiently close to be treated together.
43. It is not clear whether the ideal, self-reproducing capitalism is supposed to have in fact existed. Keane [1978] interprets this 'golden age' historically, citing Offe's *Industry and Inequality* as evidence. In effect, both Habermas and Offe often use past tense to describe it but the tone is often counterfactual. No dates or places are ever cited or used to locate this period historically. Habermas, in particular, writes in the manner of "Once upon a time, there existed liberal capitalism. . . ." In any case, the Offe-Habermas theory of state begins with the observation that none of the above is true of contemporary ("late") capitalism.
44. His evidence consists of a reference to Hobsbawm's *Age of Revolution*, which is neither here nor there.
45. This emphasis that the state replaces, not just complements, the market in contemporary capitalism and that as the consequence the law of value is no longer

valid distinguishes Habermas and Offe from the German "capital logic" school, particularly Altvater and Hirsch [in Holloway and Picciotto, 1978], who insisted that since the state cannot be a source of value, it can never replace the system of production. This difference of views had important methodological consequences: the "capital logic" school was willing to derive the structure and/or the function of the state from the historical evolution of the economy even under advanced capitalism, while Habermas and Offe insisted that the economy cannot be taken as the point of departure because the economy is organized by the state. According to Offe, "As we can no longer regard the system of political authority as a mere reflex or subsidiary organization for securing social interests, we are forced to abandon the traditional approach, which sought to reconstruct the political system and its functions from the elements of political economy" [1972b: p. 79]. Moreover, in Offe's view, marxist class analysis is useless under late capitalism since the existence of classes as political actors is not given and their organizational forms are molded by the state: "Under the conditions of late capitalism, any attempt to explain the political organization of power through the categories of political economy becomes implausible. That is to say, both sides of the politically represented class relationship become problematic under the institutional conditions of late capitalist, democratically constituted societies" [1972: p. 81] This is a recurrent theme of Offe's more recent writings, collected in 1985.

46. Note that this analysis converges almost perfectly with that of Stigler [1975], discussed in Part I. The difference is that in Offe's and Habermas' view the market is a self-destructive institution and the state must step in to save it, while in Stigler's view state intervention is not only undesirable but also gratuitous.

47. Habermas is not any more certain. For example, he writes with regard to rationality of state decisions, that "The possibility that the administrative system might open a compromise path between competing claims that would allow a sufficient amount of organizational rationality, cannot be excluded from start on logical grounds." [1975: p. 64]

48. Unless indicated to the contrary, all references to Poulantzas are to his 1973 (1968) book, *Political Power and Social Classes*.

49. For Offe [1975b: p. 9], the need for political legitimacy "emerges in capitalist society out of needs that are not satisfied through exchange processes." Habermas says explicitly that competitive capitalism was legitimate and then he wobbles on the point of for whom it was legitimate.

50. Poulantzas never bothered to specify what these activities are and how they must be organized for capitalism to be reproduced. He relied on the canonical Althusserian list of "instances" or "levels": economic, political, ideological and scientific. Althusserians eschewed the concept "society" as empiricist and preferred to speak of a "social formation," which consisted of such "levels."

51. These case studies typically began with a summary of Poulantzas' theory. Then followed a description of some cases of state intervention: the Lockheed loan, the bailing out of Rolls Royce, the origins of a welfare program, etc. The conclusion asserted that Poulantzas was right and restated the introduction. This prolific production was eventually replaced by an outpouring of case studies which began with a summary of Skocpol's critique of Poulantzas, followed by a description of some cases of state intervention, and a conclusion that Skocpol was right. I always wonder whether anyone would notice if some elf would randomly mix the stories and the conclusions.

52. Whitt [1979] provides a fascinating, but not quite convincing, example that contradicts Poulantzas' thesis.

53. For a rational choice analysis of the conditions under which particular firms would undertake collective actions see Bowman [1982, 1985].

54. Skocpol, in her Introduction to *Bringing the State Back In* discovers that states influence class formation but this is a rather belated discovery, since Luxemburg [1970] and Gramsci [1971] have both developed rather elaborate theories on this topic even before Poulantzas. I reviewed these theories in an article published in 1977.

55. Poulantzas asserts that it is a function of the capitalist state to divide workers but this language is confusing: if it is a "function," the term has a different meaning than elsewhere in his book. Capitalism just happened to be this way.

56. This was, by the way, Hempel's [1965] classical critique of functionalism.

57. Witness controversies whether Keynes' theory was known to the Swedish Social Democratic government of 1932 or the French Popular Front government of 1936.

58. Miliband cites Gramsci and used some of his terminology but both the argument that hegemony is based on the ownership of the "means of intellectual production" and the notion of hegemony as a hoax are antithetical to Gramsci's position. A similar interpretation of Gramsci was given by Anderson [1977].

59. Lindblom [1977] also tends to confuse interests of businessmen with those of business.

60. At this moment the reader may remark that this is the neo-liberal theory as well. It is. The Chicago school argues that all transfers of income cause deadweight losses and all support-maximizing governments are tempered in their zeal for redistribution by the fact that owners of endowments will withdraw them from productive uses if imposed upon. [Peltzman 1976, Becker 1983 and Bates and Lien 1985 present formal models.] The difference between the two theories is that neo-liberals are "pluralists," that is, they are agnostic about the groups which have the power of inflicting the losses on the public by withdrawing their endowments. This difference should not obscure, however, the fact that both theories understand in the same way the relation between income distribution and investment. In turn, the issue of structural dependence does not arise within the Keynesian framework in which profits and investment increase as wage rates increase.

61. This approach was, in my view, not any less "state centric" than anything that followed. The state is the center of society: society existed only because it is held together by the state. The difference between marxist state-centric theories of reproduction of capitalism and the state-centric approach of Skocpol et al. seems primarily methodological: while the first approach was frankly functionalist and implicitly teleological, the latter is militantly empiricist and contingent.

62. Przeworski and Wallerstein [1982] analyzed a solution with capitalists as a Stackelberg leader but they abandoned this solution in the 1988 article arguing that capitalists cannot solve their collective action with regard to investment. Collective leadership of capitalists with regard to wages is more credible and, in fact, wage bargaining in many countries is highly centralized on both sides. Nevertheless, in spite of the emphasis on employers' associations in the Schmitter variant of the corporatist literature, collective action by firms rarely enters either the theoretical or the empirical analyses.

63. Several modelers, for example Calmfors and Horn [1985], give up on imputing an objective to the state and begin their analyses with the reaction function. Yet this solution is unsatisfactory and unnecessary. A general function in which governments derive utility from the welfare of specific constituencies, from winning elections and from self-interest of bureaucrats is sufficient in most cases for comparative statics.

BIBLIOGRAPHY

Adler, Frank. (1979). "Thalheimer, Bonapartism and Fascism," *Telos* **40**: 70–108.
Alavi, Hamza. (1972). "The State in Post-Colonial Societies: Pakistan and Bangladesh," *New Left Review* **74**: 59–81.
Alessi, Louis De. (1969). "Implications of Property Rights for Government Investment Choices," *American Economic Review* **59**: 13–24.
Alt, James E., and K. Alec Chrystal. (1983). *Political Economics* Berkeley: University of California Press.
Althusser, Louis. (1971). "Ideology and Ideological State Apparatuses," in Louis Althusser, *Lenin and Philosophy and Other Essays* New York: Monthly Review Press.
Althusser, Louis, and Etienne Balibar. (1970). *Reading Capital* London: New Left Books.
Altvater, Elmar. (1978). "Some Problems of State Interventionism: The 'Particularization' of the State in Bourgeois Society," in John Holloway and Sol Picciotto (eds.), *State and Capital: A Marxist Debate* London: Edward Arnold.
Ames, Edward, and Richard T. Rapp. (1977). "The Birth and Death of Taxes: A Hypothesis," *Journal of Economic History* **37**: 161–178.
Anderson, Perry. (1977). "The Antinomies of Antonio Gramsci," *New Left Review* **100**: 5–78.
Arrow, Kenneth J. (1951). *Social Choice and Individual Values* New York: Wiley. (rev. ed. 1963).
Arrow, Kenneth J. (1971). "Political and Economic Evaluation of Social Effects and Externalities," in M.D. Intriligator (ed.), *Frontiers of Quantitative Economics* Amsterdam: North-Holland.
Auerbach, Alan J. (1983). "Taxation, Corporate Financial Policy and the Cost of Capital," *Journal of Economic Literature* **21**: 905–940.
Aumann, Robert J., and Mordecai Kurz. (1977). "Power and Taxes," *Econometrica* **45**: 1137–1161.
Axelrod, Robert. (1970). *Conflict of Interest* Chicago: Markham.
Bachrach, Peter, and Morton S. Baratz. (1970). *Power and Poverty: Theory and Practice* New York: Oxford University Press.
Badie, Bertrand, and Pierre Birnbaum. (1983). *The Sociology of the State* Chicago: University of Chicago Press.
Balibar, Etienne. (1970). "The Basic Concepts of Historical Materialism," in Louis Althusser and Etienne Balibar, *Reading Capital* London: New Left Books.
Ballard, C. L., J. B. Shoven, and John Whalley. (1985). "General Equilibrium Computations of the Marginal Welfare Costs of Taxes in the United States," *American Economic Review* **75**: 128–138.
Baran, Paul, and Paul Sweezy. (1966). *Monopoly Capital* New York: Monthly Review Press.
Basar, Tamer, Alain Haurie, and G. Ricci. (1985). "On the Dominance of Capitalists' Leadership in a 'Feedback–Stackelberg' Solution of a Differential Game Model of Capitalism," *Journal of Economic Dynamics and Control* **9**: 101–125.
Bates, Robert H., and D. D. Lien. (1985). "A Note on Taxation, Development and Representative Government," *Politics and Society* **14**: 53–70.
Bator, Francis M. (1958). "The Anatomy of Market Failure," *Quarterly Journal of Economics* **72**: 351–379.
Beck, Nathaniel. (1978). "Social Choice and Economic Growth," *Public Choice* **33**: 33–48.

Becker, Gary S. (1958). "Competition and Democracy," *Journal of Law and Economics* 1: 105-109.
Becker, Gary S. (1976). "Comment [on Peltzman, 1976]," *Journal of Law and Economics* 19: 245-248.
Becker, Gary S. (1983). "A Theory of Competition Among Pressure Groups for Political Influence," *Quarterly Journal of Economics* 98: 371-400.
Bennett, Douglas, and Kenneth Sharpe. (1980). "The State as Banker and Entrepreneur: The Last Resort Character of the Mexican State's Economic Intervention, 1917-76," *Comparative Politics* 12: 165-189.
Bentley, Arthur F. (1908). *The Process of Government* Chicago: University of Chicago Press.
Birnbaum, Pierre. (1985). "L'action de l'Etat," in Madeleine Grawitz and Jean Leca (eds.), *Traité de Science Politique, Vol. 3* Paris: Presses Universitaires de France.
Black, Duncan. (1958). *The Theory of Committees and Elections* Cambridge: Cambridge University Press.
Block, Fred. (1977). "The Ruling Class Does Not Rule: Notes on the Marxist Theory of the State," *Socialist Revolution* 33: 6-28.
Block, Fred. (1980). "Beyond Relative Autonomy: State Managers as Historical Subjects," in Ralph Miliband and John Saville (eds.). *Socialist Register, 1980* London: Merlin Press.
Bobbio, Norberto. (1984). *Il Futuro Della Democrazia* Torino: Eindaudi.
Borooah, V. K., and Frederick Van der Ploeg. (1983). *Political Aspects of the Economy* Cambridge: Cambridge University Press.
Bowen, H. R. (1943). "The Interpretation of Voting in the Allocation of Economic Resources," *Quarterly Journal of Economics* 58: 27-48.
Bowles, Samuel. (1985). "The Production Process in a Competitive Economy," *American Economic Review* 75: 16-36.
Bowles, Samuel, and Herbert Gintis. (1982). "The Crisis of Liberal Democratic Capitalism: The Case of the United States," *Politics and Society* 11: 51-93.
Bowman, John. (1982). "The Logic of Capitalist Collective Action," *Social Science Information* 21: 571-604.
Bowman, John. (1985). "The Politics of the Market: Economic Competition and the Organization of Capitalists," *Political Power and Social Theory* 5: 35-88.
Breton, Albert, and Ronald Wintrobe. (1975). "The Equilibrium Size of a Budget-maximizing Bureau: A Note on Niskanen's Theory of Bureaucracy," *Journal of Political Economy* 83: 195-207.
Browning, Edgar K., and William R. Johnson. (1984). "The Trade-Off Between Equality and Efficiency," *Journal of Political Economy* 92: 175-203.
Bruno, Michael, and Jeffrey Sachs. (1985). *Economics of Worldwide Stagflation* Cambridge: Harvard University Press.
Buchanan, J. M., Tollison, and Gordon Tullock, (eds.). (1980). *Toward a Theory of the Rent-Seeking Society* College Station: Texas A&M University Press.
Buchanan, Paul. (1985). *Regime Change and State Organization in Postwar Argentina* Ph.D. Dissertation. University of Chicago.
Burke, Edmund. (1984). "Thoughts and Details on Scarcity," in Marilyn Butler (ed.), *Burke, Paine, Godwin, and the Revolution Controversy* Cambridge: Cambridge University Press.
Bush, Winston C., and Robert J. Mackay. (1977). "Private versus Public Sector Growth: A Collective Choice Approach," in T. E. Borcherding (ed.), *Budgets and Bureaucrats* Durham: Duke University Press.
Calmfors, Lars, and Henrik Horn. (1985). "Classical Unemployment, Accomodation

Policies and the Adjustment of Real Wages," *The Scandinavian Journal of Economics* **87**: 234–261.

Cameron, David R. (1984). "Social Democracy, Corporatism, Labor Quiescence and the Representation of Economic Interest in Advanced Capitalist Society," in John H. Goldthorpe (ed.), *Order and Conflict in Contemporary Capitalism: Studies in the Political Economy of Western European Nations* Oxford: Clarendon Press.

Cardoso, Fernando H. (1971). *Ideologias de la burguesia industrial en sociedades dependientes: Argentina y Brasil* Siglo Veintiuno.

Cardoso, Fernando H., and Enzo Faletto. (1979). *Dependency and Development in Latin America* Berkeley: University of California Press.

Carnoy, Martin. (1984). *The State and Political Theory* Princeton: Princeton University Press.

Castles, Francis G. (1987). "Neocorporatism and the 'Happiness Index', or What the Trade Unions Get for Their Cooperation," *European Journal of Political Research* **15**: 381–393.

Cawson, Alan, and John Ballard. (1984). "A Bibliography of Corporatism," European University Institute Working Paper No. 84/115. Florence: EUI.

Chandra, Bipan. (1980). "Karl Marx, His Theories of Asian Societies and Colonial Rule," in UNESCO, *Sociological Theories: Race and Colonialism* Paris: UNESCO.

Clifton, James A. (1977). "Competition and the Evolution of the Capitalist Mode of Production," *Cambridge Journal of Economics* **1**: 137–151.

Coase, R. H. (1960). "The Problem of Social Cost," *The Journal of Law and Economics* **3**: 1–44.

Coleman, Jules. (1982a). "The Normative Basis of Economic Analysis: A Critical Review of Richard Posner's *The Economics of Justice*," *Standard Law Review* **34**: 1105–1131.

Coleman, Jules. (1982b). "The Economic Analysis of Law," in Roland Pennock and John Chapman (eds.), *Ethics, Economics and the Law* New York: New York University Press.

Coleman, Jules, and John Ferejohn. (1986). "Democracy and Social Choice," *Ethics* **97**: 6–25.

Collier, David (ed.). (1979). *The New Authoritarianism in Latin American* Princeton: Princeton University Press.

Conaghan, Catherine. (1985). "Technocrats, Capitalists and Politicians: Economic Policy Making in Redemocratized States," Unpublished Papers.

Crain, W. Mark. (1977). "On the Structure and Stability of Political Markets," *Journal of Political Economy* **85**: 829–842.

Crouch, Colin. (1985). "Conditions for Trade Union Wage Restraint," in L. N. Lindberg and C. S. Maier (eds.), *The Politics of Inflation and Economic Stagnation* Washington, D.C.: Brookings.

Dahl, Robert A. (1956). *A Preface to Democratic Theory* Chicago: University of Chicago Press.

Davis, Lance E. (1980). "It's a Long, Long Road to Tipperary, or Reflections on Organized Violence, Protection Rates, and Related Topics: The New Political History," *Journal of Economic History* **40**: 1–16.

Davis, O., and M. Hinich. (1966). "A Mathematical Model of Policy Formation in a Democratic Society," J. Bernd (ed.), *Mathematical Applications in Political Science II* Dallas: Southern Methodist University Press.

Davis, O. A., M. J. Hinich, and P. C. Ordeshook. (1970). "An Expository Development of A Mathematical Model of the Electoral Process," *American Political Science Review* **64**: 426–448.

Dixit, Avinash, and Gene Grossman. (1984) "Directly Unproductive Prophet-Seeking Activities," *American Economic Review* **74**: 1087–1088.

Domhoff, G. William. (1970). *The Higher Circles: the Governing Class in America* New York: Random House.
Downs, Anthony. (1957). *An Economic Theory of Democracy* New York: Harper and Row.
Driffill, John. (1985). "Macroeconomic Stabilization Policy and Trade Union Behavior as a Repeated Game," *The Scandinavian Journal of Economics* **87**: 300–326.
Dülffer, Jost. (1976). "Bonapartism, Fascism and National Socialism," *Journal of Contemporary History* **11**: 109–128.
Easton, David. (1965). *A Framework for Political Analysis* Englewood Cliffs, N.J.: Prentice-Hall.
Elster, Jon. (1984). *Ulysses and the Sirens: Studies in Rationality and Irrationality* Revised Edition. Cambridge: Cambridge University Press.
Elster, Jon. (1985). *Making Sense of Marx* Cambridge: Cambridge University Press.
Evans, Peter. (1979). *Dependent Development: The Alliance of Multinational, State and Local Capital in Brazil* Princeton: Princeton University Press.
Evans, Peter. (1985). "Transnational Linkages and the Economic Role of the State: An Analysis of Developing and Industrialized Nations in the Post-World War II Period," in P. Evans, D. Rueschemeyer and T. Skocpol (eds.), *Bringing the State Back In* Cambridge: Cambridge University Press.
Evans, P., D. Rueschemeyer, and T. Skocpol (eds.). (1985). *Bringing the State Back In* Cambridge: Cambridge University Press.
Ferejohn, John A. (1974). *Pork Barrel Politics* Stanford: Standford University Press.
Fiorina, Morris. (1977). *Congress: Keystone of the Washington Establishment* New Haven: Yale University Press.
Fiorina, Morris, and R. G. Noll. (1978). "Voters, Bureaucrats, and Legislators: A Rational Choice Perspective on the Growth of Bureaucracy," *Journal of Public Economics* **9**: 239–254.
Foley, Duncan K. (1967). "Resource Allocation and the Public Sector," *Yale Economic Essays* **7**: 45–98.
Foley, Duncan K. (1978). "State Expenditure from a Marxist Perspective," *Journal of Public Economics* **9**: 221–238.
Frank, Andre Gunder. (1979). *Dependent Accumulation and Underdevelopment* New York: Monthly Review Press.
Frey, B. S. (1978). "Politico-Economic Models and Cycles," *Journal of Public Economics* **9**: 203–220.
Frey, B.S., and F. Schneider. (1982). "Politico-Economic Models in Competition with Alternative Models: Which Predict Better?," *European Journal of Political Research* **10**: 241–254.
Furtado, Celso. (1963). *The Economic Growth of Brazil* Berkeley: University of California Press.
Furubotn, Eirik G., and Svetozar Pejovich. (1972). "Property Rights and Economic Theory: A Survey of Recent Literature," *Journal of Economic Literature* **10**: 1137–1162.
Garrett, Geoffrey, and Peter Lange. (1988). "Parties, Policies and Performance: The Political Economy of Economic Decline, 1974–1984," Paper presented at the Annual Meeting of the Midwest Political Science Association, Chicago, April 14–16, 1988.
Gerstenberger, Heide. (1978). "Class Conflict, Competition and State Functions," in John Holloway and Sol Picciotto (eds.), *State and Capital: A Marxist Debate* London: Edward Arnold.
Gramsci, Antonio. (1971). *Prison Notebooks* New York: International Publishers.
Greenberg, Joseph, and Shlomo Weber. (1985). "Multiparty Equilibria under Proportional Representation," *American Political Science Review* **79**: 693–703.

Griffin, L. J., J. A. Devine, and Michael Wallace. (1982). "Monopoly Capital, Organized Labor, and Military Expenditures in the United States, 1949-1976," in Michael Burawoy and Theda Skocpol (eds.), *Marxist Inquiries. Supplement to American Journal of Sociology* **88**: S113-S153.

Habermas, Jürgen. (1975). *Legitimation Crisis* Boston: Beacon Press.

Hall, Peter A. (1984). "Patterns of Economic Policy: An Organizational Approach," in S. Bornstein, D. Held, and J. Krieger (eds.), *The State in Capitalist Europe* London: Allen and Unwin.

Hamada, Koichi. (1973). "A Simple Majority Rule on the Distribution of Income," *Journal of Economic Theory* **6**: 243-264.

Harberger, Arnold C. (1954). "Monopoly and Resource Allocation," *American Economic Review, Papers and Proceedings* **44**: 77-87.

Harberger, Arnold C. (1971). "Three Basic Postulates for Applied Welfare Economics: An Interpretive Essay," *Journal of Economic Literature* **9**: 785-797.

Hempel, Carl G. (1965). "The Logic of Functional Analysis," in Carl G. Hempel, *Aspects of Scientific Explanation* New York: Free Press.

Hersoug, Tor. (1985). "Workers versus Government — Who Adjusts to Whom?," *The Scandinavian Journal of Economics* **87**: 270-292.

Hibbs, Douglas A., Jr. (1987). *The Political Economy of Industrial Democracies* Cambridge, MA: Harvard University Press.

Hibbs, Douglas A., Jr., and Heino Fassbender. (1981). *Contemporary Political Economy* Amsterdam: North-Holland.

Hicks, Alexander. (1988). "Social Democratic Corporatism and Economic Growth," *Journal of Politics* **50**: 677-704

Hintze, Otto. (1975). *The Historical Essays of Otto Hintze* Edited by F. Gilbert. New York: Oxford University Press.

Hirsch, Joachim. (1978). "The State Apparatus and Social Reproduction: Elements of a Theory of the Bourgeois State," in John Holloway and Sol Picciotto (eds.), *State and Capital: A Marxist Debate* London: Edward Arnold.

Hochman, Harold M., and James D. Rodgers. (1969). "Pareto Optimal Redistribution," *American Economic Review* **59**: 542-557.

Hoel, Michael. (1978). "Distribution and Growth as a Differential Game Between Workers and Capitalists," *International Economic Review* **19**: 335-350.

Holloway, John, and Sol Picciotto. (1978). *State and Capital* Austin: University of Texas Press.

Hotelling, Harold. (1929). "Stability in Competition," *Economic Journal* **39**: 41-57.

Jessop, Bob. (1982). *The Capitalist State: Marxist Theories and Methods* New York: New York University Press.

Joskow, Paul L., and Roger C. Noll. (1981). "Regulation in Theory and Pratice: An Overview," in Gary Fromm (ed.), *Studies in Public Regulation* Cambridge, MA: MIT Press.

Katzenstein, Peter (Ed.). (1978). *Between Power and Plenty* Madison: University of Wisconsin Press.

Keane, John. (1978). "The Legacy of Political Economy: Thinking with and against Claus Offe," *Canadian Journal of Political and Social Theory* **2**: 49-78.

Keohane, Nannerl O. (1980). *Philosophy and the State in France* Princeton: Princeton University Press.

Kleiman, Ephraim. (1983). "Fear of Confiscation and Redistribution. Notes towards a Theory of Revolution and Repression," Seminar Paper No. 247. Institute for International Economic Studies, Stockholm.

Kolm, Serge-Christophe. (1984). *La Bonne Eonomie. La Reciprocite Generale* Paris: Presses Universitaires de France.

Kramer, Gerald H. (1973). "On a Class of Equilibrium Conditions for Majority Rule," *Econometrica* **41**: 285-297.

Kramer, Gerald H., and James M. Snyder. (1983). "Fairness, Self-Interest, and the Politics of the Progressive Income Tax," Paper presented at the Annual Meeting of American Political Science Association, Chicago.

Krasner, Stephen D. (1978). *Defending the National Interest: Raw Materials Investments and U.S. Foreign Policy* Princeton: Princeton University Press.

Krasner, Stephen D. (1984). "Approaches to the State: Alternative Conceptions and Historical Dynamics," *Comparative Politics* **16**: 223-246.

Krueger, Anne O. (1974). "The Political Economy of the Rent-Seeking Society," *American Economic Review* **64**: 291-303.

Laclau, Ernesto. (1977). *Politics and Ideology in Marxist Theory* London: Verso.

Lancaster, Kelvin. (1973). "The Dynamic Inefficiency of Capitalism," *Journal of Political Economy* **81**: 1092-1109.

Lane, Frederic C. (1958). "Economic Consequences of Organized Violence," *Journal of Economic History* **18**: 401-417.

Lane, Frederic C. (1979). *Profits from Power: Readings in Protection Rent and Violence-Controlling Enterprises* Albany: State University of New York Press.

Lange, Peter. (1984). "Unions, Workers, and Wage Regulation: The Rational Bases of Consent," in John H. Goldthorpe (ed.), *Order and Conflict in Contemporary Capitalism: Studies in the Political Economy of Western European Nations* Oxford: Clarendon Press.

Lange, Peter, and Geoffrey Garrett. (1985). "The Politics of Growth: Strategic Inter-action and Economic Performance in the Advanced Industrial Democracies, 1974-1980," *Journal of Politics* **47**: 792-827.

Lazear, Edward P. (1983). "A Microeconomic Theory of Labor Unions," in Joseph D. Reid, Jr. (ed.), *Research in Labor Economics: New Approaches to Labor Unions* Supplement 2. Greenwich, CT: JAI Press.

Lembruch, Gerhard. (1982). "Neo-Corporatism and the Function of Representative Institutions," Paper presented at the Conference on Representation and the State. Stanford University.

Levi, Margaret. (1981). "The Predatory Theory of Rule," *Politics and Society* **10**: 431-465.

Leys, Colin. (1975). *Underdevelopment in Keyna. The Political Economy of Neo-Colonialism* Berkeley: University of California Press.

Lindblom, Charles E. (1977). *Politics and Markets: The World's Political-Economic Systems* New York: Basic Books.

Luxemburg, Rosa. (1970). *Reform or Revolution* New York: Pathfinder Press.

McKelvey, Richard D. (1976). "Intransitivities in Multidimensional Voting Models and Some Implications for Agenda Control," *Journal of Economic Theory* **12**: 472-482.

Malcomson, James M. (1987). "Trade Union Labour Contracts: An Introduction," *European Economic Review* **31**: 139-148.

Manley, John. (1983). "Neopluralism: A Class Analysis of Pluralism I and Pluralism II," *American Political Science Review* **77**: 368-383.

Mann, Michael. (1984). "The Autonomous Power of the State," *Archives Europeennes de Sociologie* **25** 185-213.

Marks, Gary. (1986). "Neocorporatism and Incomes Policy in Western Europe and North America," *Comparative Politics* **18**: 253-277.

Marx, Karl. (1934). *The Eighteenth Brumaire of Louis Bonaparte* Moscow: Progress Publishers.

Marx, Karl. (1952a). *Wage Labor and Capital* Moscow: Progress Publishers.
Marx, Karl. (1952b). *The Class Struggle in France, 1848 to 1850* Moscow: Progress Publishers.
Marx, Karl. (1967). *Capital* (3 vols.) New York: International Publishers.
Marx, Karl. (1971). *Writings on the Paris Commune* Edited by H. Draper. New York: International Publishers.
Marx, Karl. (1973). *Grundrisse* (Edited by M. Nicolaus. New York: Vintage Books.
Mehrling, Perry G. (1986). "A Classical Model of Class Struggle: A Game-Theoretic Approach," *Journal of Political Economy* **94**: 1280-1303.
Meltzer, Allan H., and Scott F. Richard. (1981). "A Rational Theory of the Size of Government," *Journal of Political Economy* **89**: 914-927.
Migué, Jean-Luc, and Gérard Bélanger. (1974). "Toward a General Theory of Managerial Discretion," *Public Choice* **17**: 27-47.
Miliband, Ralph. (1969). *The State in Capitalist Society* New York: Basic Books.
Miliband, Ralph. (1972). *Parliamentary Socialism* (2nd ed.) London: Merlin Press.
Miller, Gary, and Terry M. Moe. (1983). "Bureaucrats, Legislators, and the Size of Government," *American Political Science Review* **77**: 297-322.
Miller, Nicolas R. (1983). "Pluralism and Social Choice," *American Political Science Review* **77**: 734-747.
Mills, C. Wright. (1956). *The Power Elite* New York: Oxford University Press.
Morey, E. R. (1984). "Confuser Surplus," *American Economic Review* **74**: 163-173.
Morishima, Michio. (1973). *Marx's Economics* Cambridge: Cambridge University Press.
Mueller, Dennis C. (1979). *Public Choice* Cambridge: Cambridge University Press.
Müller, Wolfgang, and Christel Neusüss. (1975). "The Illusion of State Socialism and the Contradition between Wage Labor and Capital," *Telos* **25**: 13-90.
Murray, Robin. (1971). "The Internationalization of Capital and the Nation State," *New Left Review* **67**: 84-109.
Musgrave, Richard A. (1971). "Provision for Social Goods in the Market System," *Public Finance* **26**: 304-320.
Nettl, J. P. (1968). "The State as a Conceptual Variable," *World Politics* **20**: 559-592.
Niskanen, William A. (1971). *Bureaucracy and Representative Government* Chicago: University of Chicago Press.
Nordlinger, Eric. (1981). *On the Autonomy of the Democratic State* Cambridge, MA: Harvard University Press.
North, Douglass C. (1981). *Structure and Change in Economic Hisotry* New York: W.W. Norton.
North, Douglass C. (1984). "Government and the Cost of Exchange in History," *Journal of Economic History* **44**: 255-264.
O'Connor, James. (1973). *The Fiscal Crisis of the State* New York: St. Martin's Press.
O'Donnell, Guillermo. (1973). *Modernization and Bureaucratic-Authoritarianism: Studies in South American Politics* Berkeley: University of California Press.
O'Donnell, Guillermo. (1976). "Modernization and Military Coups: Theory, Comparisons, and the Argentine Case," in Abraham F. Lowenthal (ed.), *Armies and Politics in Latin America* New York: Holmes and Meier.
O'Donnell, Guillermo. (1977). *Apuntes para una teoria del Estado* Buenos Aires: CEDES.
O'Donnell, Guillermo. (1980). "Comparative Historical Formations of the State Apparatus and Socio-Economic Change in the Third World," *International Social Science Journal* **32**: 717-729.
OECD. (1983). *Positive Adjustment Policies* Paris: OECD.

Offe, Claus. (1972a). "Political Authority and Class Structures — An Analysis of Late Capitalist Societies," *International Journal of Sociology* 2: 73-108.

Offe, Claus. (1972b). "Advanced Capitalism and the Welfare State," *Politics and Society* 2: 479:488.

Offe, Claus. (1973). "The Abolition of Market Control and the Problem of Legitimacy (I)," *Kapitalistate* 1: 109-116.

Offe, Claus. (1973). "The Abolition of Market Control and the Problem of Legitimacy (II)," *Kapitalistate* 2: 73-75.

Offe, Claus. (1974). "Structural Problems of the Capitalist State," *German Political Studies* 1: 31-57.

Offe, Claus. (1975a). "The Theory of the Capitalist State and the Problem of Policy Formation," in Leon N. Lindberg et al (eds.), *Stress and Contradiction in Modern Capitalism* Lexington: Lexington Books.

Offe, Claus. (1975b). "Laws of Motion of Reformist State Policies," An excerpt from, *Berufabildungs Reform — Eine Fall Studie uber Reform Politik* Manuscript.

Offe, Claus. (1984). *Contradictions of the Welfare State* Edited by John Keane. Cambridge: MIT Press.

Offe, Claus. (1985). *Disorganized Capitalism* Edited by John Keane. Cambridge: MIT Press.

Offe, Claus, and Volker Ronger. (1975). "Theses on the Theory of the State," *New German Critique* 6: 137-147.

Offe, Claus, and Helmut Wiesenthal. (1980). "Two Logics of Collective Action: Theoretical Notes on Social Class and Organizational Form," *Political Power and Social Theory* 1: 67-115.

Ordershook, Peter C. (1986). *Game Theory and Political Theory* Cambridge: Cambridge University Press.

Orzechowski, William. (1977). "Economic Models of Bureaucracy: Survey, Extensions, and Evidence," in T. E. Borcherding (ed.), *Budgets and Bureaucrats* Durham: Duke University Press.

Oswald, Andrew J. (1979). "Wage Determination in an Economy with Many Trade Unions," *Oxford Economic Papers* 31: 369-385.

Oswald, Andrew J. (1985). "The Economic Theory of Trade Unions: An Introductory Survey," *The Scandinavian Journal of Economics* 87: 160-193.

Oszlak, Oscar. (1981). "The Historical Formation of the State in Latin America," *Latin American Research Review* 16: 3-32.

Padgett, John F. (1981). "Hierarchy and Ecological Control in Federal Budgetary Decision Making," *American Journal of Sociology* 87: 75-129.

Panitch, Leo. (1980). "Recent Theorizations of Corporatism: Reflections on a Growth Industry," *British Journal of Sociology* 31: 159-187.

Panitch, Leo. (1981). "Trade Unions and the Capitalist State," *New Left Review* 125: 21-43.

Parkinson, C. Northcote. (1957). *Parkinson's Law and Other Studies in Administration* New York: Ballentine Books.

Pashukanis, E. B. (1951). "General Theory of Law and Marxism," in V. I. Lenin et al (Translated by Hugh W. Babb, with an Introduction by John N. Hazard), *Soviet Legal Philosophy* Cambridge, MA: Harvard University Press.

Peltzman, Sam. (1976). "Toward a More General Theory of Regulation," *Journal of Law and Economics* 19: 211-240.

Peltzman, Sam. (1980). "The Growth of Government," *Journal of Law and Economics* 22: 209-287.

Pizzorno, Alessandro. (1985). "On the Rationality of Democratic Choice," *Telos* 63: 41-69.

Plott, Charles R. (1976). "Axiomatic Social Choice Theory: An Overview and Interpretation," *American Journal of Political Science* **20**: 511–527.

Poggi, Gianfranco. (1978). *The Development of the Modern State. A Sociological Introduction* Stanford: Stanford University Press.

Pohjola, Matti. (1983). "Nash and Stackelberg Solutions in a Differential Game Model of Capitalism," *Journal of Economic Dynamics and Control* **6**: 173–186.

Pohjola, Matti. (1984). "Threats and Bargaining in Capitalism: A Differential Game View," *Journal of Economic Dynamics and Control* **8**: 291–302.

Pommerehne, Werner W. (1978). "Institutional Approaches to Public Expenditures: Empirical Evidence from Swiss Municipalities," *Journal of Public Economics* **7**: 255–280.

Poulantzas, Nicos. (1964). "L'examen marxiste de l'Etat et du droit actuels et al question de ⟨l'alternative⟩," *Less Temps Modernes* **219–20**: 274–302.

Poulantzas, Nicos. (1973). *Political Power and Social Classes* London: New Left Books.

Poulantzas, Nicos. (1978). *State, Power, Socialism* London: New Left Books.

Przeworski, Adam. (1977). "Proletariat into a Class: The Process of Class Formation from Karl Kautsky's 'The Class Struggle' to Recent Controversies," *Politics and Society* **7**: 343–401.

Przeworski, Adam. (1981). "Compromiso de clases y estado: europa occidental y america latina," in Norbert Lechner (Ed.), *Estado y Politica en America Latina* Siglo Veintiuno.

Przeworski, Adam. (1985). *Capitalism and Social Democracy* Cambridge: Cambridge University Press.

Przeworski, Adam, and Michael Wallerstein. (1982a). "The Structure of Class Conflict in Democratic Capitalist Societies," *American Political Science Review* **76**: 215–238.

Przeworski, Adam, and Michael Wallerstein. (1982b). "Democratic Capitalism at the Crossroads," *Democracy* **3**: 52–68.

Przeworski, Adam, and John Sprague. (1986). *Paper Stones. A History of Electoral Socialism* Chicago: University of Chicago Press.

Przeworski, Adam, and Michael Wallerstein. (1988). "Structural Dependence of the State on Capital," *American Political Science Review* **82**: 11–29.

Rae, Douglas W. (1967). *The Political Consequences of Electoral Laws* New Haven: Yale University Press.

Rein, G. A. (1960). *Bonapartismus und Faschismus in der deutschen Geschichte* Göttingen: Musterschmidt-Verlag.

Remmer, Karen L., and Gilbert W. Merkx. (1982). "Bureaucratic-Authoritarianism Revisited," with a reply by Guillermo O'Donnell. *Latin American Research Review* **17**: 3–50.

Riker, William H. (1962). *The Theory of Political Coalitions* New Haven: Yale University Press.

Riker, William H. (1982). *Liberalism Against Populism: A Confrontation between the Theory of Democracy and the Theory of Social Choice* San Francisco: W. H. Freeman.

Roberts, Kevin W. S. (1977). "Voting over Income Tax Schedules," *Journal of Public Economics* **8**: 329–340.

Romer, Thomas. (1975). "Individual Welfare, Majority Voting, and the Properties of a Linear Income Tax," *Journal of Economic Public* **4**: 163–185.

Romer, Thomas, and Howard Rosenthal. (1979). "The Elusive Median Voter," *Journal of Public Economics* **12**: 143–170.

Rudolph, Lloyd, and Sussanne H. Rudolph. (1985). "The Subcontinental Empire and the Regional Kingdom in Indian State Formation," in Paul Wallace (ed.), *Region and Nation in India* New Delhi: Oxford and IBH.

Samuelson, Paul A. (1966). "The Pure Theory of Public Expenditure," in Joseph E. Stieglitz (ed.), *The Collective Scientific Papers of Paul A. Samuelson* Cambridge, MA: MIT Press.
Saul, John. (1979). *The State and the Revolution in Eastern Africa* New York: Monthly Review Press.
Saunders, Peter, and Friedrich Klau. (1985). *The Role of the Public Sector. Causes and Consequences of the Growth of Government* OECD Economic Studies, Special Issue (4). OECD: Paris.
Scharpf, Fritz W. (1984). "Economic and Institutional Constraints of Full-Employment Strategies: Sweden, Austria and West Germany, 1973–1982," in John H. Goldthorpe (ed.), *Order and Conflict in Contemporary Capitalism: Studies in the Political Economy of Western European Nations* Oxford: Clarendon Press.
Scharpf, Fritz. (1988). "The Political Calculus of Inflation and Unemployment in Western Europe: A Game Theoretical Interpretation," Paper presented at the Conference on the Micro-Foundations of Democracy, University of Chicago, April 29 — May 1, 1988.
Schmidt, Manfred G. (1982). "Does Corporatism Matter? Economic Crisis, Politics and Rates of Unemployment in Capitalist Democracies in the 1970s," in G. Lehmbruch and P. C. Schmitter (eds.), *Patterns of Corporatist Policy-Making* London: Sage Publications.
Schmitter, Philippe C. (1974). "Still the Century of Corporatism?," *Review of Politics* 36: 85–131.
Schmitter, Philippe C. (1977). "Modes of Interest Intermediation and Models of Societal Change in Western Europe," *Comparative Political Studies* 10: 7–38.
Schmitter, Philippe C. (1983). "Democratic Theory and Neocorporatist Practice," *Social Research* 50: 885–928.
Schmitter, Philippe C. (1986). "Neo-Corporatism and the State," in Wyn Grant (ed.), *The Political Economy of Corporatism* London: Macmillan.
Schmitter, Philippe C., and Donald Brand. (1979). "Organizing Capitalists in the United States: The Advantages and Disadvantages of Exceptionalism," Paper presented at the Annual Meeting of American Political Science Association, Chicago.
Schmitter, Philippe C., and Gerhard Lehmbruch (eds.). 1979. *Trends toward Corporatist Intermediation* Beverley Hills: Sage.
Schmitter, Philippe C., and Wolfgang Streeck. (1981). "The Organization of Business Interests. A Research Design to Study the Associative Action of Business in the Advanced Industrial Societies of Western Europe," Discussion Paper IIM/LMP 81-13. Berlin: Wissenschaftszentrum.
Schofield, Norman. (1978). "Instability of Simple Dynamic Games," *Review of Economic Studies* 45: 575–594.
Schofield, Norman. (1982). "Instability and Development in the Political Economy," in P. C. Ordeshook and K. A. Shepsle (eds.), *Political Equilibrium* Boston: Kluwer-Nijhoff.
Schofield, Norman. (1985). "Manipulation of the Political Economy," Paper presented at the World Congress of IPSA, Paris.
Schott, Kerry. (1984). *Policy, Power and Order. The Persistence of Economic Problems in Capitalist States* New Haven: Yale University Press.
Schumpeter, Joseph A. (1954). "The Crisis of the Tax State," *International Economic Papers* 4: 5–38.
Schumpeter, Joseph A. (1975). *Capitalism, Socialism and Democracy* New York: Harper.
Schwerin, Don S. (1980). "The Limits of Organization as a Response to Wage-Price Problem," in Richard Rose (ed.), *Challenge to Governance* Beverly Hills: Sage.

Schwerin, Don S. (1982). "Incomes Policy in Norway: Second-Best Corporate Institutions," *Polity* 14: 464–480.

Semmler, Willi. (1984). *Competition, Monopoly, and Differential Profit Rates* New York: Columbia University Press.

Sen, Amartya. (1977). "Social Choice Theory: A Re-examination," *Econometrica* 45: 53–89.

Shalev, Michael. (1983). "The Social Democratic Model and Beyond: Two 'Generations' of Comparative Research on the Welfare State," *Comparative Social Research* 6: 315–351.

Shapiro, Carl, and Joseph E. Stiglitz. (1984). "Equilibrium Unemployment as a Worker Discipline Device," *American Economic Review* 74: 433–444.

Shepsle, Kenneth A. (1979a). "Institutional Arrangements and Equilibrium in Multidimensional Voting Models," *American Journal of Political Science* 23: 27–59.

Shepsle, Kenneth A. (1979b). "The Private Use of the Public Interest," Working Paper No. 46. Center for the Study of American Business, Washington University, St. Louis.

Shepsle, Kenneth A., and Barry R. Weingast. (1981). "Political Preferences for the Pork Barrel: A Generalization," *American Journal of Political Science* 25: 96–111.

Shepsle, Kenneth A., and Barry R. Weingast. (1984). "Political Solutions to Market Problems," *American Political Science Review* 78: 417–434.

Silberberg, Eugene. (1978). *The Structure of Economics. A Mathematical Analysis* New York: McGraw-Hill.

Silberman, Bernard. (1982). "The Bureaucratic State in Japan: the Problem of Authority and Legitimacy," in T. Najita and J. V. Koschmann (eds.), *Conflict in Modern Japanese History* Princeton: Princeton University Press.

Skidelsky, Robert (ed.). (1977). *The End of the Keynesian Era: Essays on the Disintegration of the Keynesian Political Economy* New York: Holmes and Meier.

Skidelsky, Robert. (1979). "The Decline of Keynesian Politics," in Colin Crouch (ed.), *State and Economy in Contemporary Capitalism* London: Croom Helm.

Skocpol, Theda. (1980). "Political Response to Capitalist Crisis: Neo-Marxist Theories of the State and the Case of the New Deal," *Politics and Society* 10: 155–201.

Skocpol, Theda. (1985). "Bringing the State Back in: Strategies of Analysis in Current Research," in P. Evans, D. Rueschemeyer, and T. Skocpol (eds.), *Bringing the State Back In* Cambridge: Cambridge University Press.

Soederstroem, Hans Tson. (1985). "Union Militancy, External Shocks and the Accomodation Dilemma," *The Scandinavian Journal of Politics* 87: 335–351.

Stepan, Alfred. (1978). *The State and Society: Peru in Comparative Perspective* Princeton: Princeton University Press.

Stepan, Alfred. (1985). "State Power and the Strength of Civil Society in the Southern Cone of Latin America," in Peter Evans, D. Rueschemeyer and T. Skocpol (Eds.), *Bringing the State Back In* Cambridge: Cambridge University Press.

Stigler, George. (1970). "Director's Law of Public Income Redistribution," *Journal of Law and Economics* 13: 1–10.

Stigler, George. (1972). "Economic Competition and Political Competition," *Public Choice* 13: 91–106.

Stigler, George. (1975). *The Citizen and the State. Essays on Regulation* Chicago: University of Chicago Press.

Streeck, Wolfgang. (1984). "Neo-Corporatist Industrial Relations and the Economic Crisis in West Germany," in John H. Goldthorpe (ed.), *Order and Conflict in Contemporary Capitalism: Studies in the Political Economy of Western European Nations* Oxford: Clarendon Press.

Strinati, Dominic. (1979). "Capitalism, the State and Industrial Relations," in Colin

Crouch (ed.), *State and Economy in Contemporary Capitalism* London: Croom Helm.
Stuart, Charles. (1984). "Welfare Costs per Dollar of Additional Tax Revenue in the United States," *American Economic Review* 74: 352-362.
Supple, Barry. (1973). "The State and the Industrial Revolution, 1700-1914," in C. M. Cipolla (ed.), *The Fontana Economic History of Europe, Vol. 3: The Industrial Revolution* London: Collins-Fontana Books.
Suzumura, Kotaro. (1983). *Rational Choice, Collective Decisions, and Social Welfare* Cambridge: Cambridge University Press.
Thalheimer, August. (1979). "On Fascism," *Telos* 40: 109-122.
Tilly, Charles. (1985). "War Making and State Making as Organized Crime," in P. Evans, D. Rueschemeyer, and T. Skocpol (eds.), *Bringing the State Back In* Cambridge: Cambridge University Press.
Tingsten, Herbert. (1973). *The Swedish Social Democrats* Totowa, NJ: Bedminster Press.
Tollison, Robert D. (1982). "Rent Seeking: A Survey," *Kyklos* 35: 575-602.
Trimberger, E. (1978). *Revolution from Above: Military Bureaucrats and Development in Japan, Turkey, Egypt and Peru* New Brunswick, N.J.: Transaction Books.
Truman, David B. (1951). *The Governmental Process* New York: Alfred A. Knopf.
Van den Doel, Hans. (1979). *Democracy and Welfare Economics* Cambridge: Cambridge University Press.
van der Ploeg, F. (1987). "Trade Unions, Investment, and Employment: A Non-Cooperative Approach," *European Economic Review* 31: 1465-1492.
Wallerstein, Michael. (1984). "The Micro-Foundations of Corporatism: Formal Theory and Comparative Analysis," Paper presented at the Annual Meeting of American Political Science Association, Washington, D.C.
Wallerstein, Michael. (1988a). "Union Growth from the Union's Perspective: Why Smaller Countries Are More Highly Organized," Working Paper No. 149, Institute of Industrial Relations, University of California, Los Angeles.
Wallerstein, Michael. (1988b). "The Structural Dependence of the State on Internationally Mobile Capital," Unpublished Manuscript.
Wallerstein, Michael, and Adam Przeworski. (1988). "Union Power and Union Militancy," Paper presented at the Annual Meeting of the American Political Science Association, Washington, D.C., August 1988.
Ward, Benjamin. (1982). "Taxes and the Size of Government," *American Economic Review, Papers and Proceedings* 72: 346-350.
Weber, Max. (1968). *Economy and Society* New York: Bedminster Press.
Weingast, Barry R. (1979). "A Rational Choice Perspective on Congressional Norms," *American Journal of Political Science* 24: 245-263.
Weingast, Barry R., and Mark J. Moran. (1983). "Bureaucratic Discretion or Congressional Control? Regulatory Policymaking by the Federal Trade Commission, *Journal of Political Economy* 91: 765-800.
Whitt, J. A. (1979). "Can Capitalists Organize Themselves?," *Insurgent Sociologist* 9: 51-59.
Wiatr, Jerzy J. (1987). *Marksizm I Polityka* Warszawa: Ksiazka i Wiedza.
Wilensky, Harold L. (1981). "Leftism, Catholicism, and Democratic Corporatism: The Role of Political Parties in Recent Welfare State Development," in Peter Flora and A. J. Heidenheimer (eds.), *The Development of Welfare States in Europe and America* New Brunswick: Transaction Books.
Williamson, Oliver E. (1964). *The Economics of Discretionary Behavior: Managerial Objectives in a Theory of the Firm* Englewood Cliffs, NJ: Prentice-Hall.
Wirth, Margaret. (1975). "Contribution à la critique de la théorie du capitalisme

monopoliste d'Etat," in J. -M. Vincent et al., *L'Etat contemporain et le marxisme* Paris: Maspero.

Wittman, Donald A. (1973). "Parties as Utility Maximizers," *American Political Science Review* **67**: 490–498.

Wittman, Donald A. (1983). "Candidate Motivation: A Synthesis of Alternative Theories," *American Political Science Review* **77**: 142–157.

Wolf, Charles, Jr. (1979). "A Theory of Nonmarket Failure: Framework for Implementation Analysis," *Journal of Law and Economics* **22**: 107–139.

Wolfe, Alan. (1981). "Sociology, Liberalism, and the Radical Right," *New Left Review* **128**: 3–27.

Wood, Gordon S. (1969). *The Creation of the American Republic, 1776–1787* Chapel Hill: University of North Carolina Press.

Wright, John R., and Arthur S. Goldberg. (1985). "Risk and Uncertainty as Factors in the Durability of Political Coalitions," *American Political Science Review* **79**: 704–718.

Young, L. (1982). "Comment," in J. N. Bhagwati (ed.), *Import Competition and Response* Chicago: University of Chicago Press.

Ziemann, W., and M. Lanzendörfer. (1977). "The State in Peripheral Societies," in Ralph Miliband and John Saville (eds.). *Socialist Register, 1977* London: Merlin Press.

INDEX

125

For Product Safety Concerns and Information please contact our
EU representative GPSR@taylorandfrancis.com Taylor & Francis
Verlag GmbH, Kaufingerstraße 24, 80331 München, Germany